PIVOTAL STRATEGIES FOR THE EDUCATIONAL LEADER

The Importance of Sun Tzu's The Art of War

Ovid K. Wong

Rowman & Littlefield Education
Lanham, Maryland • Toronto • Plymouth, UK
2008

Published in the United States of America
by Rowman & Littlefield Education
A Division of Rowman & Littlefield Publishers, Inc.
A wholly owned subsidiary of
The Rowman & Littlefield Publishing Group, Inc.
4501 Forbes Boulevard, Suite 200, Lanham, Maryland 20706
www.rowmaneducation.com

Estover Road
Plymouth PL6 7PY
United Kingdom

British Library Cataloguing in Publication Information Available

Library of Congress Cataloging-in-Publication Data

Wong, Ovid K.
  Pivotal strategies for the educational leader : the importance of Sun Tzu's
The art of war / Ovid K. Wong.
    p. cm.
  Includes bibliographical references.
  ISBN-13: 978-1-57886-740-0 (hardcover : alk. paper)
  ISBN-10: 1-57886-740-1 (hardcover : alk. paper)
  ISBN-13: 978-1-57886-741-7 (pbk. : alk. paper)
  ISBN-10: 1-57886-741-X (pbk. : alk. paper)
 1. Educational leadership–Philosophy. 2. School management and
organization–Philosophy. 3. Sunzi, 6th cent. B.C. Sunzi bing fa. I. Title.
  LB2805.W56 2008
  371.2001–dc22   2007035984

This book is dedicated to Ada, my wife,
for her encouragement and patience to keep me on task.

CONTENTS

LIST OF FIGURES AND TABLES

FIGURES

TABLES

FOREWORD

Dr. Wong's use of *Sun-Tzu's the Art of War* in discussing educational leadership is not the first time this ancient Chinese classic has been employed to illuminate situations in modern times. There have been similar applications to other realms of human endeavor, such as management, business, and how to be successful in one's personal life. An Internet search will unearth a plethora of examples, as well as numerous more traditional military literatures. Nevertheless, Dr. Wong's work is the first of its kind to integrate a prominent Eastern philosophy with the application of educational leadership in the Western world.

How is it that this kind of ancient wisdom can still thrive and make a contribution today, and why is Sun Tzu's work particularly relevant in the area of leadership? Reduced to its essentials, as in the recent Sawyer edition (*The Essential Art of War*, 2005), the book is reminiscent of other Taoist classics such as *I Ching* and even the *Tao te Ching*. In spite of what many commentaries may lead one to believe, Sun Tzu's wisdom is a core of concepts and principles. It is the relevant application of these concepts and principles that explains the continued vitality and popularity of the *Art of War*.

Some clues to the nature of the book may be found in the opening pages. According to Sun Tzu, warfare should be "structured" according

xii   FOREWORD

to "five winning factors": the Tao, Heaven, Earth, Generals, and the
Methods of Military Organization and Discipline. The Tao is a part of
"general wisdom" about how to live and conduct one's affairs so as to be
in harmony with life and the universe. The Tao "causes people to be
fully in accord with the ruler. Thus they will die with him; they will live
with him and not fear danger" (this and the remaining quotes in this
paragraph are all from chapter 1 in Sawyer). This refers to unity of mind
of the people when they feel they are serving a higher purpose. "Heaven
encompasses *yin* and *yang*, cold and heat, the constraints of the seasons,
going with and going contrary to, the basis of victory in warfare." This
refers to having spontaneous, intuitive understanding of natural forces
and energies, natural and human, physical and mental, and the natural
rhythms of these and connections between them. Victory is based on the
balance of going with and going contrary to these, on understanding
how one's own task and plan fits in with these. "Earth encompasses high
and low, far or near, difficult or easy, expansive or confined ground, ten-
able or fatal terrain"; this refers to aspects that naturally affect the outcome, that one has to accept and that cannot be changed, and that one
also has to go with and sometimes contrary to. These kinds of things are
also dealt with in *I Ching,* etc.

The reason the *Art of War* is especially applicable to leadership in organizational and institutional settings becomes apparent from the last
two factors. "The general encompasses wisdom, credibility, benevo-
lence, courage and strictness," and has other characteristics such as tran-
quility, uprightness, disdain for fame, and devotion. It is the combination, the unity of these partly conflicting qualities in the individual, that
characterizes a leader: benevolent and strict, wise and courageous, credible to all the members of the organization, capable of making right decisions under trying circumstances, successful in the long run. "The
Laws of Military Organization and Discipline encompass organization
and regulations, the Tao of command, and the management of logistics."
So the *Art of War* addresses squarely the situation of the individual who
is leading a large organization of many people in a large task, who faces
both the objective conditions (materials, information, etc.) and the mental (feeling and moral) factors involved in trying to attain the goal, who
deals with both the state of large aggregates and the situation at the level
of the individual, and so on. Again and again the book stops and ex-

claims: The general who is such and such will be victorious, the one who isn't such and such, won't. "[The generals] who understand the five factors will be victorious. Those who do not understand the five factors will not be victorious."

Dr. Wong does a very good job explaining that the success of a school leader is not based only on the possession of knowledge and skills. To be successful, the leader has to integrate his or her knowledge and skills with the factors of Heaven and Earth. One can witness the frustration of an aspiring school administrator when the operation is based in isolation on what he or she knows and can do.

Not all the major themes in the *Art of War* will necessarily illuminate leadership in education today (e.g., Sun Tzu advocates "deception" as a major technique). There is, however, one strand that runs wide and deep through the whole book that is likely to be very important to a modern reader. The reader constantly hears the voice of a person who has largely risen above his emotions and desires and is not much subject to them, who is aware of the large-scale factors and aggregate situation just as much as he is of the forces affecting each individual member of the organization, and who, in spite of the fact that sometimes great hurt to a large number of people is unavoidable, has a broad human outlook. One focus of the book is the emphasis on self-knowledge that goes beyond knowledge of one's own strengths and weaknesses: "One who knows the enemy and himself is not endangered in a hundred engagements"; "in antiquity, those who excelled in warfare first made themselves unconquerable in order to await the moment when the enemy could be conquered. Being unconquerable lies with yourself, being conquerable lies with the enemy." Repeatedly, the *Art of War* asserts the preservation of men and resources and the minimum total destruction of the enemy as the highest excellence. "Attaining one hundred victories in one hundred battles is not the pinnacle of excellence. Subjugating the enemy army without fighting is the pinnacle of excellence." It is the combination of this self-knowledge and overall humanistic outlook, found also in the wisdom literature of other traditions, that endows the book with uncommon objectivity and clarity and a sense of freedom.

Some time ago I was meeting with a graduate student in one of my classes who, as an early research project, was interviewing the vice president of a large company, a woman, about how she was able to occupy such a high position in the company and be at the same time a mother to her children. This was the first interview the student had conducted with her (several more were planned), and the aim was primarily to get a sense of the major outlines of the participant's situation. As I read the transcript and as we listened to the tape, an amazing story unfolded. Twenty odd years ago the participant, who is now a vice president in her fifties, was working in a grocery store as a checker. She knew she was good with numbers and did not want to work in that position forever but did not have much confidence. However, encouraged by her friends at work, she went to junior college to get a diploma in accounting and then joined the company as an entry level accountant. From then on, every year or two a new opportunity arose at a somewhat higher level of responsibility in another department. Each time it was a story of her seizing the opportunity with its many new challenges; unerringly sizing up and then handling the various political, business, and other aspects of the new situation; and in this way, constantly acting courageously, becoming more and more aware of herself and the nature of the business.

Much of the success of this aspiring woman could be discussed in terms of the five winning factors and the whole spirit of the *Art of War*. And yes, it became perfectly clear how this woman, on her path to the position she is in now, was at the same time a beautiful mother: With the same spirit and natural intuitive abilities she relied on to rise in the company, she also inspired and led her family.

The relevance of the ancient literature is as much part of humanity today as when it was written in 500 B.C. Any additional reflective effort to bring these modes of insight and awareness closer to the modern world, as represented by Dr. Wong's book, are very welcome.

Klaus Witz, Ph.D.
Professor, College of Education
University of Illinois at Urbana-Champaign

INTRODUCTION

Bing *Fa* (*Art of War* in English) was written more than 2,500 years ago by Sun Tzu, a Chinese military strategist. The text was written at approximately the time when Socrates and other philosophers were developing Western philosophy as we know it today. The *Art of War*, less than 6,000 words long, is a very complex work of philosophy and military strategy. A good part of the *Art of War* describes the pivotal role of a leader and his understanding and application of the "winning factors."

The *Art of War* is paradoxical in that, despite its title, it opposes wars and conflicts if they can be avoided. Sun Tzu explained that to overcome the enemy without fighting is the best of all strategies. Many people understand war as a fight between two or more opposing groups involving soldiers and weapons. The opposing group is often called the enemy: someone who hates and harms you. Sun Tzu used these definitions of *war* and *enemy* in his work. However, revised definitions of *war* and *enemy* are in order for application of the *Art of War* strategies in education, which is not in the literal context of fighting someone who hates and harms you. The *Art of War* strategy in education is about solving (i.e., fighting) problems (i.e., the enemy) to improve student and school success.

Public education has been criticized profusely in recent years for the underachievement of schools. One key catchphrase for long-term school success is "school leadership." Taken comprehensively, leadership emphasizes the importance of where the leader stands at times of decision, challenge, and conflict. The *Art of War* describes the significance of a leader and his or her knowledge and prudent application of specific strategies. At the core of these strategies is the non-negotiable moral purpose of the leader, reinforced by other fine leadership qualities such as wisdom, commitment, discipline, and courage.

The *Art of War,* in many translations, has now reached the corners of the world. The book can be used to resolve conflicts: within oneself, between two individuals, between armies, and between political organizations or countries. The reader will be surprised as well as rewarded by the relevance and applicability of this ancient Eastern philosophy to the Western world of education today.

THE RELEVANCE OF SUN TZU

Throughout recorded history there seems to have been a pressing need to understand and win in human conflicts. Many great military leaders have been studied and emulated because of their success in such conflicts, including such figures as Alexander the Great, Hannibal, Quinn Chi, Julius Caesar, Genghis Khan, Attila the Hun, Napoleon Bonaparte, Admiral Horatio Nelson, General Robert E. Lee, Chief Joseph of the Nez Percé, Geronimo, General George Patton, and General Dwight D. Eisenhower.

It has been more than two millennia since the brilliant Chinese military strategist Sun Tzu created and practiced his principles of warfare, the *Art of War*. His insights on human nature in conflict are encapsulated in his great work for our perusal. For decades we have repeatedly reincarnated Sun Tzu's wisdom to address the challenges of modern-day conflicts. Sun Tzu's principles of warfare are both insightful and applicable to the present-day human interactions that span many levels of our social and psychological fabric.

Copies of the *Art of War* date from antiquity, and they confirm Sun Tzu's authorship. In 1972, an archaeological dig in a second-century tomb in Silver Sparrow Mountain in Shantung, China, unearthed a cache of manuscripts with inscriptions in bamboo strips matching the work of Sun Tzu. Sun Tzu's works were long studied in Asia and were brought to the West in the 1700s. Over the past 200 years, many generals have read Sun Tzu's work and have applied his theories to their wars. The works of Sun Tzu have been widely known in the United States since the mid-1970s; their principles of conducting warfare have been the subject of serious study in U.S. military circles for many years. Henry Kissinger, secretary of state (1973–1977) under President Richard Nixon, has made reference to Sun Tzu. The *Art of War*, as applied to business, sports, diplomacy, and personal lives, has been popularized in American business and management texts, not so much as cryptic wisdom but more as pure and simple common sense. It is not surprising that Sun Tzu is frequently quoted worldwide.

In more recent years, the *Art of War* philosophies have gone Hollywood and influenced the making of movies. Yoda, the wise old Jedi Master introduced in the first *Star Wars* trilogy, is based on the *Art of War* philosophies. The influence of Sun Tzu's thinking in the Jedi Warrior philosophies is deliberate. In inventing "The Force," the moviemaker borrowed from Sun Tzu's "The Way," a force that connects all life and the way things are in the universe. To demonstrate the influence of Sun Tzu's teachings in the Jedi philosophy, replace "the Force" with "the Way" in the following sentence: "Those who act in accord with the Force, will succeed; those that act against the Force will find only peril"; the sentence could easily appear in any of the *Star Wars* movies!

WHO WAS SUN TZU?

Sun Wu (later changed to Tzu) lived in the sixth century BC, during the chaotic "Warring States" period, long before the first unified Chinese empire was formed. Recorded history is scant for the period of the construction of the Great Wall. Finding any official records about Sun Wu during his time is difficult. Nevertheless, an early biography is found in *Shih Chi (History Record)*, the first comprehensive written history of China, authored by Ssu-ma Chien (145–85 BC), the emperor's grand historian. This record, written about 350 years after Sun Tzu's time, reported that Sun was the family name and Wu the given name. (Wu was later replaced by Tzu, a title given to honor him as a great master, sim-

ilar to people today using such titles as president or prime minister.) Sun
Tzu's family was a clan of experts in arms and war strategies. His teachings are a combination of his clan's ideas and his own, as well as concepts
influenced by early Taoism. Ssu-ma Chien gave us a dramatic anecdote
about Sun Tzu and his work, *Bing Fa* (the *Art of War*).

As a young man, Sun Wu was already politically inclined. His interest
was based on the ideal of unifying the divided warring states, regardless
of the victory or defeat of the feudal lords. He understood that victory
was the consequence of many factors. He studied battle records, visited
old battlefields, and analyzed the information he acquired to create a
new way of thinking, a theory about effective war strategies. These
strategies later became the *Art of War*.

It has been said that Sun Wu was surveying an old battlefield to
study the terrain in an attempt to understand how the commander
used the landscape when maneuvering his soldiers. In the midst of the
survey, there was a heavy downpour. Sun Wu quickly took cover in a
nearby abandoned pavilion that arched right over a small beautiful
creek. The rainstorm lasted the whole morning. Sun Wu had nothing
better to do during the deluge, so he looked around, enjoying the rainy
scenery. The continuous downpour ran off the ground and spilled into
the creek. As Sun Wu observed the rising creek water, he saw that the
fast-moving water created new paths of flow. What was interesting to
Sun Wu was that the rushing water seemed to flow around the bedrock
of the creek and take a path through the loose sediment that had little
cover from the ground vegetation. Sun Wu carefully took note: The
flowing water was the force; the rocks were the resistance to the force;
and the water followed a path of loose soil, which had the least resistance to the gushing force. Sun Wu carefully wrote down these observations and his interpretation.

This field record later became an important part (sections III and VI)
of the *Art of War*. "The best policy is to attack while the enemy is still
planning. The next best is to disrupt alliances. The next best is to attack
the opposing army. The worst is to attack the enemy's city . . . "
(Gagliardi 2003). Stubborn resistance, such as that of hard bedrock or a
walled city, is not the best choice in an engagement. Breaking the enemy's resistance without fighting is the supreme goal and is considered
to be the epitome of war strategies.

The *Art of War* brought Sun Tzu to the attention of the emperor of that time. The emperor read the book with great interest and asked Sun Tzu if his military theory could be put to a test, and asked further if the strategies could be applied to women. Sun Tzu assured the emperor that they could. To test this assertion, the emperor brought 180 women from the palace. Sun Tzu quickly divided the women into an army with two troops, using the king's favorite concubines as the captains of each troop.

Sun Tzu's directions to the troops were straightforward. He instructed the women to take the four cardinal positions of front, back, left, and right. He asked them to follow simple drill orders, such as eyes front, left turn, right turn, and about turn. The women agreed to the rules and expectations. Then, to the sound of battle drums, Sun Tzu gave the order "right turn." The women thought that was funny, and they broke out giggling. Sun Tzu said that if orders were not followed, then the directions might not be clear, and the commander was to blame. The drill was resumed, and this time Sun Tzu gave the order "left turn." Again the women broke out giggling. Sun Tzu repeated that if the orders were not followed, then the directions might not be clear, and the commander was to blame. However, if the orders were clear but not followed, then the captain was to blame. Swiftly, he ordered the execution of the two captains. The emperor, watching the drill intensely from a distance, was startled by Sun Tzu's directive, and he quickly came to the rescue. The emperor said he was quite satisfied with Sun Tzu's military ability, and pleaded that the captains' lives be spared. Sun Tzu replied that serving as the supreme commander to the emperor, he could not grant the request. Accordingly, he ordered the execution of the two captains and appointed two replacements. When this had been done, the battle drum rolled one more time, and the drill resumed. This time, the troops swiftly followed the directions, with great precision. They went through the various drill maneuvers without uttering a sound.

Sun Tzu then presented the troops to the emperor for a final inspection, saying that the soldiers were properly trained, disciplined, and ready to go through thick and thin unquestioningly. The emperor was greatly shaken by the execution of the two concubines and said that he had no desire for the inspection. Sun Tzu was not thrilled by this lukewarm response. He retorted that the emperor was not serious about the request to test his military theory. The emperor realized that Sun Tzu was not only well versed in military training but also committed to getting the job done.

It was recorded that the emperor later appointed Sun Tzu supreme commander of his imperial army. During his military career, Sun Tzu defeated neighboring states with his great military skill and spread fear among the feudal warlords. Sun Tzu won many battles and shared the might and glory of the emperor.

In the *Art of War*, Sun Tzu revealed much of his training and experience in leading an army to victory. Figure 1.1 contains various aphorisms from Sun Tzu. Do you see any direct or indirect relationships between the *Art of War* and the wisdom of an effective leader?

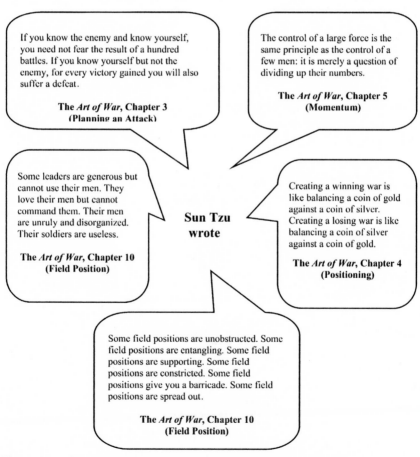

If you know the enemy and know yourself, you need not fear the result of a hundred battles. If you know yourself but not the enemy, for every victory gained you will also suffer a defeat.

The *Art of War*, Chapter 3 (Planning an Attack)

The control of a large force is the same principle as the control of a few men: it is merely a question of dividing up their numbers.

The *Art of War*, Chapter 5 (Momentum)

Some leaders are generous but cannot use their men. They love their men but cannot command them. Their men are unruly and disorganized. Their soldiers are useless.

The *Art of War*, Chapter 10 (Field Position)

Sun Tzu wrote

Creating a winning war is like balancing a coin of gold against a coin of silver. Creating a losing war is like balancing a coin of silver against a coin of gold.

The *Art of War*, Chapter 4 (Positioning)

Some field positions are unobstructed. Some field positions are entangling. Some field positions are supporting. Some field positions are constricted. Some field positions give you a barricade. Some field positions are spread out.

The *Art of War*, Chapter 10 (Field Position)

Figure 1.1. Selected Wisdom of Sun Tzu about Military Leadership

WHAT IS THE *ART OF WAR?*

The *Art of War* is a thirteen-section document originally inscribed in Chinese on bamboo strips more than 2,500 years ago. Each section can be studied individually, but more can be gained by focusing on the complete work. An English translation of the work was completed in 1905. The *Art of War* reflects Sun Tzu's philosophy and its application, which made him the outstanding military genius of his time. His words of wisdom depict the traits of a highly effective commander. Sun Tzu loves brevity of expression, but the meaning is always profound. Whether the subject be marching an army, maneuvering soldiers, estimating the enemy, or controlling the forces of victory, it is always thoroughly philosophized and explained.

An overview of the *Art of War* (see Table 1.1) is in order before further discussing the core concepts relevant to common educational practices. The thirteen sections are (1) "Analysis," (2) "Going to War," (3) "Planning an Attack," (4) "Positioning," (5) "Momentum," (6) "Weakness and Strength," (7) "Armed Conflict," (8) "Adaptability," (9) "Armed March," (10) "Field Position," (11) "Types of Terrain," (12) "Attacking with Fire," and (13) "Using Spies."

In "Analysis," Sun Tzu describes the importance of planning and strategy. Leaders plan carefully before they take action. They anticipate possible problems and prevent them from happening. In the *Art*

Table 1.1. Overview of the *Art of War*

Section	Title	Concept
1	Analysis	Assessment and planning before action
2	Going to War	Economics of warfare
3	Planning an Attack	Conservation; win without fighting
4	Positioning	Formation, adaptability, and inscrutability
5	Momentum	Force based on unity and coherence
6	Weakness and Strength	Yin and yang adaptation according to the opponent
7	Armed Conflict	Information and preparation
8	Adaptability	Adaptation based on readiness
9	Armed March	Maneuvering armies in different ways
10	Field Position	Tactical maneuvering and adaptability
11	Types of Terrain	Detailed treatment of terrain and adaptation
12	Attacking with Fire	Incendiary attack and plea for humanity
13	Using Spies	Effective use of espionage

of War, five factors are assessed: the moral law, heaven, earth, the commander, and method and discipline. This section continues to stress the three facets of the warrior's art: the social, physical, and psychological contributions.

"Going to War" discusses the economy of warfare, stressing the avoidance of prolonged warfare and the continuous depletion of resources. According to Sun Tzu, the goal of warfare should be a clever, speedy victory, not a mindless, lengthy campaign. The use of prolonged warfare will wear down the offensive as well as the defensive forces by diminishing the spirits of the troops and the supporting resources. In addition, Sun Tzu says to reward bigheartedly to motivate soldiers and reinforce their desire to defeat the enemy.

"Planning an Attack" emphasizes the significance of victory without fighting as the best strategy. The highest goal of generalship is to foil the enemy's plan; the next strategy is to prevent the connection of the enemy's forces; the next is to attack the enemy in the field; and the worst is to assault a fortified, walled city. Supreme excellence in battle is attained by breaking the enemy's resistance without bloodshed. A victory is sure to follow if a commander leads the troops wisely, makes calculated decisions about when to advance and when to retreat, works with both the sovereign and the troops, and instills high spirits in the ranks.

In "Positioning," Sun Tzu underscores the significance of taking appropriate offensive and defensive positions. The skilled general in the defensive mode hides in the secret recesses of the earth. On the other hand, the skilled general in the attack mode strikes from the topmost heights of heaven. Notice the importance of and difference between the positions of defense and attack; one is in the recesses (a low position) and the other is at the highest point of the terrain. Battles are won more by stratagem than by isolated, brute force attacks. Effective military methods include measurement, estimation, calculations, and weighing the chances of victory and defeat. A skilled general consciously modifies his tactics to meet and exceed the opposing forces, and the keys to victory are adaptability and inscrutability. By seeing opportunities before they are seen by others and responding quickly, the commander can take situations by the horns before matters get out of hand.

"Momentum" combines the use of strategies and resources to create new maneuvers and synergism. The commander uses the dynamic structure of the group and swings them into action. The crux of the teaching here is unity and coherence of an organization, and to relying on synergy rather than the qualities of any single individual. Two beautiful analogies are used: the wonderful combination of musical notes and colors. There are not more than five musical notes, yet the combinations of these five notes give rise to more melodies than can ever be heard. There are not more than five primary colors, yet in combination they produce more hues than can ever be seen. When put together under the command of a strategic, creative leader, small forces can become a large, unified force that achieves victory.

"Weakness and Strength" describes the importance of attacking the enemy's weak points with unpredictable tactics. Key to winning a battle is to avoid what is strong and strike what is weak. Military strategies are similar to flowing water, following the path of least resistance. Flowing water also shapes its course according to the nature of the ground over which it flows. Similarly, the general should strategize in relation to the opposing enemy: The path of least resistance is the enemy's weaknesses. An army, like water, has no constant formation. The ability to achieve victory by changing and adapting to the opponent is genius.

In "Armed Conflict," Sun Tzu discusses concrete field organization and combat maneuvers. Beginning with good information and preparation, the commander sets realistic and attainable goals for the troops. Sun Tzu explains that if the army marches 50 miles to battle, it will lose the leaders of the first division, and only half of the army will reach the goal. If the army is marched 30 miles with the same objective, two-thirds of it will arrive. The leader should use a variety of appropriate communication and timing strategies to make the maneuvering of a million soldiers like that of a single man. In the field of battle, the spoken word does not carry far enough; hence gongs, drums, banners, and flags are used.

"Adaptability" covers the importance of using various tactics to meet the requirements of different situations and positions. When in difficult country, the army should not encamp. In country where high roads intersect, they should join hands with their allies. The army should not linger in dangerously isolated positions. If hemmed-in, the leader should resort to stratagem. If cornered in a desperate position, the army must fight. Troops should be on the watch for inappropriate behaviors of the commander, such as recklessness, cowardice, a hasty temper, fragility of honor, and over-solicitude for the men. These inappropriate behaviors will lead to defeat.

"Armed March" explains the advantages and disadvantage of marching soldiers over various terrain. Here, "terrain" can be a metaphor for the warrior's art in dealing not only with the physical but also the social and the psychological environments. The terrain includes rivers, marshes, mountains, and plains. The army should not advance to meet the enemy in midstream when it crosses a river in its onward march. Half of the enemy should be allowed to get across, and then the attack should be launched. The leader must look for signs of the enemy advancing or retreating and be prepared to respond decisively. The rising of birds in their flight is the sign of an ambush. Startled beasts indicate that a sudden attack is coming. Soldiers must be trained in discipline and humanity. If soldiers are punished before they have grown attached to the general, they will not be submissive. Soldiers are practically useless unless they are submissive and follow the commander's orders. There must be a balance of power between the commander and the soldiers to produce harmony. If the commander regards the soldiers as his children, they will follow him into the deepest valleys; if he looks on them as his own beloved sons, they will stand by him even unto death. Only with such harmony can battles be won.

In "Field Position," Sun Tzu focuses on gaining knowledge of the ground before engaging in battle. This is a continuation of adaptability and tactical maneuvering. The ground is closely connected to the earth principle. The terrain can be accessible ground, entangling ground, tempo-rising ground, narrow passes, precipitous heights, or positions at a great distance from the enemy. With regard to narrow passes, if the army can occupy them first, they should be strongly garrisoned and should wait there for the enemy. Should the enemy forestall the army in occupying a pass, it should not go after the enemy if the pass is fully garrisoned, but rather only if it is weakly garrisoned. One essential point of discussion in this section is the relationship of the enemy to the configuration of the material, social, and psychological environments.

"Types of Terrain" pinpoints the application of a variety of tactics depending on the situation. It is a more detailed discussion of the terrain. Again, the situations can be interpreted to mean not only simple physical ground, but also the ground in its social and more abstract senses. Sun Tzu describes nine types of ground and the corresponding military positions, as well as a variety of tactics suitable for each. The nine types of ground are dispersive ground, facile ground, contentious ground, open ground, ground of intersecting highways, serious ground, difficult ground, hemmed-in ground, and desperate ground. The skilful command of an army may be likened to the behavior of a *shuai-jan*, a native snake of the Ch'ang Mountains. Strike at the snake's head, and you will be attacked by its tail. Strike at the snake's tail, and you will be attacked by its head. Strike at its middle, and you will be attacked by both the head and the tail.

"Attack with Fire" advises the use of the fire offensive only when conditions are favorable. An attack by fire involves using the right resources, coordinated with making the right decisions. For example, the army will suffer as much as its enemy if it starts a fire on the east side and attacks the enemy from the east while the wind is blowing east. Despite the fact that fire can be used as the most vicious form of martial art, it is in this section that a plea for humanity is made, that weapons are recognized as tools of misfortune and are to be used only when unavoidable.

In "Using Spies," Sun Tzu spotlights the use of espionage to get information about the enemy so that a strategic strike can be made at the right time and place. This information gained is a part of the foreknowledge of the enemy's dispositions that the commander uses to win a war. Understanding the enemy's strengths and weaknesses enhances the commander's ability to make the right decisions. An army without intelligence is like a man without ears and eyes.

A cursory reading of the *Art of War* often results in the assumption that victory is attained mainly by aggression. This assumption is incorrect. After reviewing the thirteen sections of the book and synthesizing the ideas, one would find that victory by aggression is only the last option when other solutions have failed. An analogy between the medical arts and martial arts explains why aggression should be used only as a last resort. The medical and martial disciplines are far apart in content; nevertheless, they are parallel in dealing with disharmony and conflict conceptually. In both, the understanding of a problem is key to its solution, and prevention is better than cure. In Sun Tzu's thesis, foiling the enemy's plan is similar to keeping healthy and avoiding getting sick. Foiling the alliances of an enemy is similar to staying away from contagious diseases. Engaging the enemy with armed force is more aggressive and is similar to taking medicine. Finally, performing surgery is a very aggressive approach and is like besieging the opponent's fortified, walled city. Sun Tzu would certainly advise medical doctors to help people stay healthy rather than operating on them to fix a problem that is already too serious.

Winning without fighting can also be applied to education. Fighting illiteracy and compensating below grade-level reading are common classroom practices, and unfortunately playing catch-up with student learning is the reality of the game. A K–12 school superintendent has put it best: "If students can read at grade level by the time they complete grade 3, then we will not have to play catch-up and can simply allow the natural progression of learning to move forward without fighting."

WISDOM OF THE PAST

History is a record of victories and defeats. We should learn from history or fall victim to its repetitive nature! The fear of repeating defeats or negative events conjures our emotions. Such events may include meeting the Four Horsemen of the Apocalypse: War, Famine, Pestilence, and Death. From another perspective, however, what we learn from history can also be the key to our survival and the vision for a future in which we can thrive.

How do we capture the wisdom of the past and make it relevant? Is it possible for us to understand who we are today in relation to who we were yesterday? What are the philosophical underpinnings that link the past and present intercourse of human experiences? What is the common ground of military leadership (as witnessed by the writings of an ancient Chinese military commander) that connects with today's educational leadership? In the following chapters, we systematically explore the answers to these questions.

APPLICATIONS FOR TODAY AND BEYOND

Why is Sun Tzu's *Art of War* still relevant in today's society? For one thing, warfare seems inherent in all humankind and, it goes without saying, is a phenomenon not yet facing extinction. When we take a break from warring with our neighbors in foreign lands, we turn inward to war on drugs, poverty, and hunger, then turn back again, to shadow fighting with terrorism, religiosity, imperialism, and a host of other "isms." From the very onset of our recorded history, we have studied and made war against our neighbors and ourselves, as if fear and aggression were inherent in our souls. Although warfare may not be indicative of our primordial origin, it is certainly a learned behavior that has become very much ingrained in our human interactions. As a species, we cogently nurture our instinct for warfare. We enjoy and instill competition in games, movies, stories, recreation, norms, ideologies, and our cultural mores; in sum, in our collective human psyche.

What is the connection between Sun Tzu's *Art of War* and education? There is no question that Sun Tzu devised winning methodologies for defeating the enemy on the battlefield. But within his principles of warfare Sun Tzu incorporated philosophies of knowing: oneself;, the enemy; the natural environment (heaven and earth); human nature and its strengths and weaknesses; and the alliances people make. All these "knowings" become determinants of how we think and help us to rationalize the world around us, and if analyzed accurately, they can lead to a combined knowledge and predictions of victory or defeat. From a 2,500-year perspective, we can view Sun Tzu's success on the battlefield as a result of his keen reflection on the commander and observations on the nature of the environment, which illuminated a profound wisdom about the nature of who we humans are when fear and aggression take the lead in embattlement.

Very profound in Sun Tzu's observations is that he deems the greatest leader or general of all to be the one who wins the battle without releasing the energy contained within the tension in the bowstring . . . in other words, without firing a shot.

The teachings of the *Art of War* do not place unnecessary emphasis on warfare. Rather, Sun Tzu takes the view that victory or defeat is more like the contention of psychological states. One does not need to overcome an enemy by brute force but can achieve victory by disconcerting the enemy. Remove the enemy, and its leader and nation will move from a state of harmony to one of chaos, effectively defeating it. Mahatma

Gandhi (1869–1948), a highly respected political and spiritual leader of India, fought to end discrimination against the country's minorities. He used nonviolent resistance to what he regarded as unjust laws. His methods of nonviolent civil disobedience were adopted by protagonists of civil rights in the United States and by many protest movements throughout the world. Martin Luther King Jr. (1929–1968) led a boycott of segregated city bus lines; in 1956, he achieved a major victory and prestige as a civil rights leader when Montgomery buses began to operate on a desegregated basis. King was an outstanding civil rights leader, waging war against racial inequality without violence. Both Gandhi and King exemplify Sun Tzu's philosophy of winning without fighting.

Sun Tzu was both a master military strategist and a political strategist. He both advised and warned emperors about the efficacy of waging war, exemplifying means for them to think strategically. He calculated the skill level of opposing generals, the capabilities and needs of armies and individuals alike, as well as the importance of finance and resources and building networks of communication at varying levels. Sun Tzu was meticulous in his observance of the physical, societal, and psychological worlds surrounding him. He mastered strategic thinking, and his philosophical blend of knowledge-based observation was definitive in his ability to predict outcomes of battles and political conflict. These valuable abilities Sun Tzu attributed to the focused wisdom gained through his observations of heaven and earth and the moral purpose. He warned that the outcome of loss occurs when a commander fails to understand the nature of all things.

What could be more relevant to education by today's standards than to better understand "the balance in the nature of all things"? Our children's future depends on the effectiveness of our nation's educators and their leadership. Our society needs our leading advocates for education to be on the cutting edge, have vision, and declare victory in a war against limitations on knowledge, or ignorance if you will. The relevance of the *Art of War* for educators is the timeless observation, knowledge, and wisdom about who we are and how we behave in times of conflict. How we define our battles and our wars is directly related to how we define our collective knowledge, and beyond that, our wisdom, with regard to a more global, social or moral code in the twenty-first century.

Chapter 2 of this book focuses on the factors and forces that prevail in today's educational battles. We discuss the timing (heaven), the landscape (earth), the administrator (the commander), his or her philosophy (moral purpose), and his or her practices (method and discipline) that lead the school to win the campaign of learning for all students. We use the five factors as the basis for discussion and connect real school experiences to reflect their application.

Chapter 3 exemplifies today's educational leader as one who effectively makes use of relevant data and research by carefully calculating strategies that will lead to educational success, such as learning for all students. The combination of strategies and resources is a synergistic process (an art form) that can lead schools to victory. Exemplary leaders today, as in the past, manage their troops wisely, keep spirits high, and know when and how to engage for ultimate success.

Chapter 4 focuses on present-day politics and reassures Sun Tzu's philosophy regarding the effectiveness of winning battles by stratagem rather than brute force. As water flows down the path of least resistance, leaders can shape the ground and ultimately prepare the course through which the water flows. Skilled visionary educational leaders consciously modify Sun Tzu's tactics to meet the needs of students and all student service providers. They set realistic and achievable goals for students and educators based on current best practice and resources.

Chapter 5 stresses the importance of clear communication from a leadership position and throughout the organization. In real estate, it is location, location, location. In leadership communication, there can never be enough information that cannot be stated enough ways. If information is not clear, concise, and repetitive, then others are likely to implement their own infomercials. Disseminate the information and ask for timely feedback regarding understanding and support of the communication. Information acquisition is critical. Information limitations are equal to knowledge limitations: Successful educational leaders network to acquire accurate information, from politics to educational strategies, in an all-inclusive effort to enhance educational success of all students. Educational leaders must be progenitors of organizational mission and vision, leading to goals, followed by initiatives and assessment of the implementation. Exceptional leaders celebrate success with their troops and avoid failure, reinventing new strategies from the lessons learned.

Chapter 6 assesses an individual's educational leadership skills based on a framework of Sun Tzu's operationally, philosophically, and politically based venues. Using observation and interpretation in combination with the art of strategy, educational leaders can make significant predictions about moving their organizations through change. Forecasting success in education takes into account adapting to rough terrain, dealing with the school board, and becoming an effective administrator in collaboration with the school community, including teachers, parents, and politicians.

In chapter 7, Sun Tzu's quotes are summarized with reference to the book chapter in which they appear and the major concepts they represent, and the reader is asked to fill in an action log that asks, "How might I apply this in my work?" Until knowledge and skills are applied, what has been read and learned will not be internalized.

Finally, we need not define war in terms of poverty, hunger, drug addiction, or terrorism. Neither are these battles, but rather, challenges that all present-day societies must face. We need not declare war on our neighbors or ourselves. Instead, if there must be war, let us define it with just cause . . . a direct result of our negligence in coming to grips with knowing ourselves. Knowing ourselves is key, as it was for Sun Tzu 2,500 years ago, to being victorious. Sun Tzu's philosophy indicates that we need to have an accurate view of ourselves if we are to be empowered with wisdom. If we are able to accomplish this much, then from a Sun Tzu perspective, observing the balance between heaven and earth and human nature, we can provide ourselves with the wisdom necessary to prevail in a battle in which wisdom will win over ignorance.

REFERENCES

Gagliardi, Gary. 2003. *The* Art of War *Plus the Ancient Chinese Revealed.* Clearbridge Publishing.

2

THE WINNING FACTORS

Your skill (as a leader) comes from five factors.
Study these factors when you plan war.
You must insist on knowing your situation.
Discuss philosophy.
Discuss the climate.
Discuss the ground.
Discuss leadership.
Discuss military methods.

(Gagliardi 2003, ch. 1)

In the *Art of War*, Sun Tzu described five factors to be taken into account when seeking to determine the conditions of the battlefield: philosophy, climate, the ground, leadership, and military methods. In essence, the five factors are interpreted as the moral purpose, the timing, the location, the commander, and the methods executed by the commander. Sun Tzu wrote that to plan for a war, the commander must know and use the five factors well. In an attempt to better understand the five factors and their hierarchical relationship, the order has been modified here from the original presentation (see figure 2.1). The diagram places the moral law as a deep-seated factor influencing all other

INTERNAL FACTORS **EXTERNAL FACTORS**

1. Moral Law (philosophy) 4. Climate (timing)

2. Commander (leadership) 5. Ground (location)

3. Methods

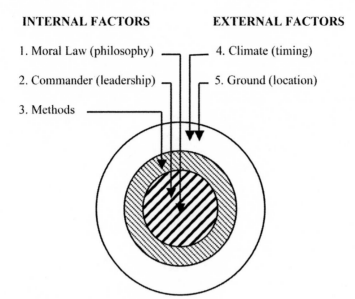

Figure 2.1.   The Five Winning Factors

leadership practices. In other words, the way the leader holds and interprets the moral law affects his or her interactions with the environment (i.e., climate, ground, method, and discipline).

THE MORAL LAW

It starts with your military philosophy.
Command your people in a way that gives them a shared higher purpose.
You can lead them to death.
You can lead them to life.
They must never fear danger or dishonesty.

(Gagliardi 2003, ch. 1)

The moral law emerges from the same social environment as some of the Chinese classics in humanism. This includes *Tao-te-Ching* (the *Book of the Way*), which was a definite philosophical influence on Sun Tzu's work. The moral law in Sun Tzu's time was defining the moral purpose

of going to war. The *Art of War* pinpoints anger and greed as fundamental causes of defeat. It is the calm, emotionally detached warrior
who wins, not the egocentric, hotheaded vengeance seeker or the ambitious fortune hunter.

It all starts with the military philosophy of the commander. A successful general commands in a way that gives the troops a higher shared
purpose. The commander orders his soldiers to charge but also explains
to them why. With only a few exceptions, the mission for going to war
cannot be classified information. Are the soldiers defending the land because an enemy has invaded their home turf? Are they fighting in a foreign land to expand their country's territory? The motivation to fight in
each of these situations is very different. The commander must not underestimate the motivation driven by the power of the moral law. The
moral law critically influences what is important or not and determines
the soldiers' possibilities for victory. It has a profound philosophical
meaning that goes beyond a mere set of rules and regulations. It concerns the truth, the right, the wrong, the nature, and the meaning of life.
The moral law, though perceived as being abstract, can be found in our
daily lives.

Imagine that you are sitting by a swimming pool and a child is drowning. You do not know exactly what has happened, and the lifeguard is
nowhere in sight. What would you do? It depends. Are you a good swimmer? It would be foolish to jump into the pool if you cannot swim. After all, there is a difference between being foolish and being brave. Under what circumstances would you jump into the pool to save the
drowning child? Would you save the child anyway if he or she were your
friend's child, or your own? When the drowning child is your own, there
is little doubt that you would risk your life to rescue him or her. This scenario provides an interesting glimpse into how we uphold the moral law.
The question that one asks is about the purpose of the sacrifice regardless of whether the decision maker in question is a swimmer. What we
know is that people are more than willing to sacrifice if they see the wor-
thiness of the cause.

As an educational leader, how would you set moral standards for yourself and the organization? What constitutes the moral law of a school can
be discerned by answering the following questions:

1. What is the primary purpose of a school?
2. What does a school represent?
3. Why did you enter the education profession?

The purpose of these questions is to create and focus on an organizational meaning, as well as self-meaning, for the existence of the organization and the profession. A recent report on a state prison found that the majority of inmates are functional illiterates with low literacy skills. What message does this send to educators? As educators, do we prepare our students for the real work world, or do we teach them to save them from going to prison? What are the options when we fail children? Or do we have any options? A careful examination of these questions will give us a sense of urgency about our moral purpose as professionals working in the field of education.

The National Policy Board for Educational Administration clearly presents standards for educational leaders and defines developing a vision that promotes the success of all students as the top priority. To realize this vision, the board further recommends that educational leaders articulate, implement, and steward the vision of learning and seek support from the school community. We can be confident that the appropriate development and the faithful execution of a vision are heavily influenced by the moral law governing the leader of the organization.

Thorough self-examination is important for understanding the moral law that we as educational leaders represent. Understanding what one stands for, what one truly believes in, what one is willing to sacrifice all for, and what one is unwilling to compromise anything for is universally characteristic of the truly great leaders of all times. Socrates referred to this concept of moral law as the most important of philosophical underpinnings.

A school superintendent, upon assuming his new role, asked, "Tell me about my predecessor. What was he like?" The response was, "Oh, he was very well liked. You have some big shoes to fill." As time passed, the new superintendent had a great deal of questions, which were asked of a wide variety of people, such as, "Why are so many of the school policies out of date? Why are so many educational programs not in place?" Not long after, the school board began complaining to the new superintendent about some administrators who were slacking off and not doing their jobs. When questioned, these administrators responded that whenever they gave directives or initiated any significant change, the teachers would complain and file grievances. Because no one really wanted to make any ripples in the pond, everyone took a laid-back approach, doing business as usual. Now that the school board was finally fed up and wanted the new superintendent to take action, a different story began to emerge. After some time, stories were told in jest about the comical side of the former superintendent, whom everyone loved. It seems that on more than one occasion, he fell asleep at his desk, not bothering anyone. As the new superintendent began strategic planning sessions with the board and began implementing change initiatives, the breadth and width of these stories intensified. It seemed as though the philosophy of the sleeping giant only met the needs of some of the troops and few of the children. Change was imminent, but the situation was extremely tenuous for the new superintendent.

Now this story could have come to a happy ending, but in reality the new superintendent, faced with so much resistance, moved on to another position. The school district hired another superintendent, and much of the administrative staff quickly reverted back to sleeping giant status. Today, the students' achievement remains mediocre. What can we say about the moral purpose of the new superintendent? How does it differ from that of the retired superintendent?

In a similar story shared by a colleague, she was attending a staff development training session sponsored by the state department of education. The program was focused on current information about student assessment and implementation of the No Child Left Behind Act. This workshop was for superintendents across the state. One superintendent slept through the entire presentation. He was awakened only by the applause at the end. He got up and left. Could you have guessed the moral purpose of the sleeping superintendent? (No, he was not the same person as in the previous story.)

Sloth and laziness is not a dominant characteristic among the ranks of today's educational leadership. However, leading from a position of integrity, as the protector of the state, as the defender of the educational law of the land, and as the primary leader, a model of the mean-

ingful educational reformer in the interest of the children, is unfortunately a rarity.

Why is it that more educational leaders don't take the moral high
ground to uphold the moral law? The answer, unfortunately, is that not
doing so is a learned behavior. Educational leaders have been attacked
resoundingly by politicians, the media, and the teachers' unions. A most
profound characteristic of the human species is that we are all emphat-
ically resistant to change. As true educators, we want—no, demand—
that our students change, yet we maintain steadfast resistance to change
within ourselves and our educational systems and institutions. The politics of America's educational institutions, from community school
boards, unions, and teachers to educational leadership, is steeped in a
climate of counterproductivity. The educational leader has become the
antireform victim . . . the poster child for scapegoating the problems of
the institution.

Educational leaders have no one to blame but themselves. The whip-
ping boy analogy exemplifies administrative or management characteristics, but not those of leadership, for a true leader sets the agenda and
leads. What is leadership if not setting the course and taking the troops
where they are unable to take themselves? We have withered in the face
of adversity. We have failed to articulate the higher sense of purpose.
We have not held the moral high ground by defining and insisting on the
best possible education for all children. We have failed to lead our
schools, our communities, and our nation to a more productive, practical, useful, and beneficial educational outcome for all of us. For the
state, as Sun Tzu would say. We have failed to take whole with regard to
educating our citizenry. Thomas Jefferson would surely say that our de-
mocracy, if not in jeopardy, is certainly being held hostage.

Those educational leaders who truly possess the skills, characteristics,
and qualities described by Sun Tzu find themselves with fewer opportunities to grow and lead for the higher cause and a sense of purpose.
The ideology that so strongly suppresses educational reform in our society is like a sovereign who has hobbled his army. Resistance to change
comes from local politicians, teachers, other administrators, and the
unions, who actively seek blood from both administrators who advocate
for change as well as those who resist change. No one can feel safe in an

educational administrative position today. War has been declared on administration by staff, the unions, and weak, politically influenced local school boards. So, although it appears at first glance that those administrators who assume a low profile with teachers and the union experience a longer tenure in their administrative positions, the reality is that the moment they are faced with adversity, when they are forced to make a decision that appears out of the ordinary, angry, change-resistant educators, political advocates, or media propagandists strike back with fury. A school leader can ride the fence for a while, but he or she will get knocked off sooner or later . . . guaranteed.

Ah! But with all this adversity, turmoil, chaos, unrest, and uncertainty, isn't this a breeding ground from which true leaders emerge? A leader must choose which side of the fence he or she will jump off to. At this time you must know who you are, what you stand for, and what you are willing to die for (figuratively speaking), for sooner or later they will aim to kill you for what you believe in. Take the high ground and advocate for the benefit of our children.

In today's world, an individual's skills and characteristics are often viewed as separate lineages. Characteristics, as if inherent, are often ascribed as xnhilo (from the Latin, out of nowhere), yet virtuous nonetheless. On the other hand, skills are often assumed to be either inherent or learned. This is an extremely important factor for today's educational leaders, for if all that is of importance in this life cannot be learned, then it will indeed be difficult for us to defend the business of teaching and learning as most important to the state.

All of what we have come to know about our earth, our universe, and ourselves we have learned through teaching, and all that we know can be passed on to future generations. We are what we know, and what we know is what we are able to learn. Even witch doctors take on apprentices. There is an anticipated risk for the educational leader who cannot find balance in this concept of learning. Let us look at an example in special needs education. In assigning the label *learning disabled*, the individual student is assessed for both IQ (inherent knowledge) and academic achievement (knowledge learned). In today's educational model, we then proceed to teach the child what he or she doesn't already know. At the other end of the spectrum, we test to identify gifted and talented students and for college potential using only IQ and assume . . . what? Potential? Or is it that we assume that much of what is needed to be known is already contained within?

In reality, in today's educational system we practice gatekeeping. We have elitism; we have tracking, bifurcated teaching methodologies, and inadequate measures of student and educator performance alike. Purpose and direction are sometimes questionable. The primary goal of keeping children in school as opposed to having them on the street is too simplistic. We must have a higher purpose, a higher goal.

In the spirit of effective leadership, both the general of Sun Tzu's era and today's modern educational leader (as perhaps can be said of all significant leaders of all times) must lead with a high moral purpose. An educational leader must be the spokesperson for the higher ideals of our society. He or she must articulate a higher sense of purpose for society and how to reach higher levels of commitment and achievement through knowledge and understanding. Today's educational leader must not only lead by the given standards of our day but also define and articulate these standards. In fact, it is leadership that redefines the standards of our time in terms and dimensions to adapt to or initiate change and a new direction.

During the past decade, a new view of the school leader emerged in the United States, a view that refocuses leadership on its primary mission of teaching for learning and student success. The driving force behind this vision of leadership has been the establishment of standards for school administrators (Hessel and Holloway 2001). A typical standard statement will be something like, "A school administrator is an educational leader who promotes the success of all students by acting with integrity, with fairness, and in an ethical manner." This statement, in Sun Tzu's words, is the moral law. The statement requires the administrator to demonstrate a personal and professional code of ethics, to understand his or her impact on the school and the community, to respect the rights and dignity of all, and to inspire integrity and ethical behavior in other people.

Finally, in the spirit of upholding the moral law through the five winning factors of Sun Tzu, it is more important to do the right thing and to instill a high purpose than to just do things right in an organization!

THE COMMANDER

> Next is the commander.
> He must be smart, trustworthy, caring, brave and strict.
>
> (Gagliardi 2003, ch. 1)

The military commander is responsible for moving the troops to attack, to retreat, or to defend a position. To make a critical decision such as this involves critically weighing the pros and cons of various factors. Figure 2.1 describes the impact of the heaven and earth factors on the possibilities of winning or losing a battle. To further complicate the decision-making process, the commander has to blend in his or her own personality. The factors may favor the commander moving to the next position. However, the final decision making may end up uncertain if the commander is a low risk taker. Hesitation is a good example of a tug-of-war between making a critical decision and the personality of the decision maker.

An effective leader has many fine qualities. Among these is being brave. In the absence of bravery, a leader, or anyone, cannot practice any other virtue with consistency. Bravery can be defined as behaving in accordance with one's own values, beliefs, and mission in the face of fear, failure, and potential loss. This definition helps us reinforce the strong connection between a person's moral purpose and his or her virtue. The bravery or courage of two school leaders is compared in the following discussion.

Recently, a newspaper ran a special report titled "A Tale of Two Schools." The two schools are located at the opposite ends of a town. North School is in a poor neighborhood, with a heavy minority student population. South School, on the other hand, is located in the affluent section of town, and the student population is mixed. From a purely socioeconomic standpoint, one would forecast student success in South School, because socioeconomic status is often used by social scientists as a predictor of student success. To find out if this hypothesis was correct, newspaper reporters visited and compared the schools. A reporter stopped by the main office of each school and interviewed the principals about the school's daily operations and their vision for the schools.

Mrs. Brown is the principal of North School. Her style of conducting school business is sincere and open. Her decision making relies on
broad-based input from the school community through teacher committees, the parent–teacher association, and the student council. She
is not intimidated by staff not going along with her ideas. Instead, she
encourages staff members to take calculated risks to improve the
school. She is moving forward to try new ideas and do new things to
improve students.

Ms. Smith is the principal of South School. She operates the school
with the close assistance of her secretary and a team of trusted teachers.
She rarely delegates beyond her immediate group because she fears that
some of the veteran teachers are more resourceful and might outma-
neuver the administration. Ms. Smith is not open to new ideas and
avoids potential conflicts. Her lack of courage and trust in people did
not bring the faculty and staff together cohesively in South School.

At the conclusion of each principal's interview, the reporter requested
to see a copy of the school report card. To the pleasant surprise of the
reporter, North School overcame the socioeconomic adversity of the
community and outperformed South School in student attendance,
graduation, and student achievement on the high-stakes state test.
There were, of course, a whole host of other factors affecting the
school's success. The success of North School points to the courage of
the North School principal. The school leader takes risk by inviting ideas
and trusting and working with staff to ensure success for all students.
The principal successfully deals with staff over confrontation. She over-
comes the fear of feeling insecure as an isolated school administrator at
the top of the organizational pyramid.

METHOD AND DISCIPLINE

> You have your military methods.
> They shape your organization.
> They come from your management philosophy.
> You must master their use.
>
> (Gagliardi 2003, ch. 1)

The way in which a commander manages the army is a part of the method and discipline described in the *Art of War*. To be effective, the commander relies first on the internal factors of moral purpose and leadership style and second on external factors such as timing and location of the situation for guidance. Sun Tzu underscores the importance of military methods because they shape the effectiveness of the organization.

It was well known in ancient China that a general had led three platoons of soldiers against a huge enemy. The army of soldiers was separated from the enemy by a river. The six battalions of enemy soldiers who camped two miles from the river were well fed and equipped. It was clear to the general that his army was outnumbered and had little chance to win. His men might face annihilation the next day when they crossed the river. The general did not for a moment think about retreat, because that was not an option. That night the general ordered the soldiers to cross the river under the cloak of a dark and misty sky. After the crossing, and before the soldiers were ready to march again, the general gave the order to break all the cooking pots and sink the boats. The order was followed, and two days later the general led the army to a great victory. Consider the mindset and the strategy of the general that were responsible for the victory. The reason for the victory was certainly not the size of the army, or the might of the fierce weapons. It was the courage, the deployed method, and discipline. When the cooking pots and boats were destroyed, the soldiers could not think about cooking another meal or recrossing the river, much less a retreat, until they fought to victory. The only chance for them to see another day was to advance, fight, and win!

Educational leadership is not restricted to the principal's office or the administration of the central office. It is alive and well in classrooms. The fact that one has an education degree does not automatically make one an effective teacher. A teacher needs to know and practice a whole host of skills and methods, and the first thing a teacher needs to know is how to manage a classroom full of students. To manage a class means to organize students, space, time, and materials so that teaching and learning can take place. In this situation, isn't the school teacher like the leader of an army, managing the soldiers and getting them ready to win the next battle?

Dr. Yen is a veteran principal of Oak Hill Middle School. Two weeks into the new school year, she is already diligent in visiting classrooms, supervising teaching and learning. Mr. Rodriquez and Ms. Michael are new to the school, and they both teach eighth-grade mathematics. On the first day that Dr. Yen visited Mr. Rodriquez's class, the students were working. They seemed to know the assignment based on the objectives written on the chalkboard, and they knew that tests are based on the stated lesson objectives. Mr. Rodriquez started the class promptly, and he went right into teaching the lesson. He spent time practicing the classroom procedures until they became routine. He knew how to praise deeds and encourage the students. On the second day, Dr. Yen visited Ms. Michael, right across from Mr. Rodriquez's classroom. Ms. Michael was working at her desk; she told the class to read chapter 4 on the theory of algebraic equations and that they would be tested on the reading. When students broke class routines, she made up rules and punished them according to her mood. Ms. Michael told the class about the rules and procedures but did not rehearse them. She used generalized student praise or none at all.

The methods and discipline implemented by Mr. Rodriquez and Ms. Michael are different. As a consequence of these different methodologies, one class is perceived by Dr. Yen as well-managed. Which one is it? A well-managed class has four characteristics. The first is a high level of student involvement with work. The second characteristic is clear expectations for both teachers and students. The third is students being on time and on task. Relatively little time is wasted on nonlearning behaviors. The fourth characteristic is a class atmosphere of respect that is conducive to learning. An effective leader is also an effective manager. Which teacher seemed to have the methods and discipline to manage the class well? Is it Mr. Rodriquez or Ms. Michael? Would you be surprised to find that the teaching philosophy (moral purpose) of the two teachers is different?

HEAVEN

Next, you have the climate.
It can be sunny or overcast.

It can be hot or cold.
It includes the timing of the seasons.

(Gagliardi 2003, ch. 1)

Climate is a symbol of the environment, with special reference to timing. The temperature and the light of the day fluctuate with the time of the day and the four seasons of the year. In ancient warfare, the most favorable time for a battle was when there was plenty of daylight and favorable temperatures for maneuvering the army over land.

How is climate or timing a critical determinant in an educational decision? Let us consider two different school districts. The River East and River West districts are both budget-bound. Budgetary limitations cause the districts to be unable to replace dated textbooks and buy new student computers. A solution for getting more revenues for these expenditures is to increase local tax dollars. The two school districts propose to raise taxes in a local referendum for education. On closer examination, there is a difference between River East and River West. River East is a performing school district. The students score above the nation's average on the ACT examination. The high school graduation rate of River East is 97.5 percent. River West, on the other hand, is an underachieving district with students scoring way below the nation's ACT examination average. The high school graduation rate is 79.5 percent. If we were to consult Sun Tzu and ask for his advice on a tax referendum for the school districts, what would he recommend? Based on the winning factor of heaven, Sun Tzu would say that the timing for proposing a tax referendum for River East is favorable. As a taxpayer for River East, is it more likely that you would dig deeper into your pocketbook to help a performing school in your own community?

As a decision maker in education, do you know when to propose an idea and gain support? What are the options if you need to make a proposal, knowing that it will not get support from your colleagues? How does cause come into the mix when making a popular versus an unpopular decision?

Another type of climate is that of the workplace. After all, the amount of daylight, the range of temperatures, wind, and clouds are contributing elements of climate. In today's work world, we often talk about the office climate with reference to moral and work productiv-

ity. According to a Harvard University researcher, the size of pay-
checks is not nearly as important as how young college professors get
along with their colleagues (*Chronicle* 2006). In this research, professors were asked in a survey to assess different climate factors in the
workplace. These factors included collegiality with other members of
the department. "Collegiality" encompassed working well with other
professors, unity of the department, level of professional interaction,
and overall job satisfaction. The respondents who answered favorably
to the survey indicated that they fit well in the department, were
treated fairly compared to one another, and would take the current position again, and well as that the administration was supportive, they
felt valued and respected in their jobs, and there was a feeling of unity
and cohesion among faculty. One respondent mentioned that good
teaching was valued over mere publication.

All in all, the various climate factors create an atmosphere that fosters
collegiality and productivity. Have you experienced a work environment
that was stressful and hostile, versus another one that was cordial and
cohesive? Would you choose one over the other at the expense of the
size of your paycheck? Why or why not? As a school leader, do you feel
that you are responsible for and have control over the climate of your organization? How would you promote harmonious climate, as interpreted by Sun Tzu, as night and day, cold and heat, times and seasons?

EARTH

> Next is the terrain.
> It can be distant or near.
> It can be difficult or easy.
> It can be open or narrow.
> It also determines your life and death.
>
> (Gagliardi 2003, ch. 1)

Ancient warfare was bound by the terrain or ground of the landscape,
including the distance that the army had to march to be engaged. The
terrain was further determined by the openness of the land. An open
landscape provided a better view of the enemy. The obstruction of high

grounds and mountains, on the other hand, hid the opposing force. The effective movement of soldiers across the landscape determined the possibilities of victory. Terrain, as interpreted by Sun Tzu, is the location and the ground that helps to define a position, a winning position. A winning position is one that will protect us from the enemy. Hold the position and wait for the right opportunity to move forward for the win.

In 480 BC, an alliance of Greek city-states fought the invading Persian Empire at the pass of Thermopylae in central Greece. This is known as the Battle of Thermopylae. At the time, the Thermopylae pass consisted of a narrow road along the shore of the Gulf of Malis that only one chariot at a time could pass over. On the southern side of the track stood the cliffs, while on the north side was the gulf. Along the path was a series of constrictions, or "gates" (pylai), where the Greeks dug in their heels.

Vastly outnumbered, the Greeks held back the Persians for three days, in one of history's most famous last stands. A small force led by King Leonidas of Sparta blocked the only road over which the massive army of Xerxes of Persia could pass. The Persians ultimately succeeded in taking the pass but suffered heavy losses, extremely disproportionate to those of the Greeks. The fierce resistance of the Spartan-led army gave Athens precious time to prepare for a decisive naval battle that would determine the outcome of the war. The subsequent Greek victory at the Battle of Salamis left much of the Persian Empire's navy destroyed, and Xerxes was forced to retreat back to Asia. The performance of the soldiers at the battle of Thermopylae is often cited by historians as an example of the advantage of good use of terrain (Sun Tzu's earth) to maximize an army's potential.

Many teachers are up against teaching in an environment of overcrowded classrooms. Effective teaching hinges on the number of students or the size of the class. How can one determine the appropriate class size or teacher–student ratio to bring forth the best of what the teacher can deliver? A number of factors determine the appropriate class size for creating the best possible learning environment. Most people would seriously consider resources (including teacher remuneration) as the major determining factor. However, the terrain factor is inherent in the determination. The landscape in Sun Tzu's time is analogous to the layout of a classroom. Let's not forget that the teacher or teaching assistant working in the classroom is also a part of the classroom layout. Other variables being equal, how would you lay out the classroom to maximize student learning? In Jefferson North High School, an administrative policy reads: "The Board [board of education] and the Association [teachers' union] agree that class size is a significant factor for teachers. Careful planning is essential to provide the best possible learning environment. For that reason, a class size of up to 20 is recommended for a class with basic skills students. A class size of up to 27 is recommended for regular students, and a class size of up to 30 is recommended for honors students."

How is the ground factor related to what we decide and do in education? Let us review a construction proposal for Lincoln Elementary School. Lincoln Elementary has a student enrollment of 1,052, with a projection of adding 300 more students over two years. The superintendent of schools and the board of education are proposing a new school construction program to accommodate the growing student population. The school has sufficient money to build an addition to the existing structure, and the superintendent consults an architectural firm. Should the school expand its facilities horizontally or vertically? The land surveyor reports that the school campus is landlocked by a lagoon to the north, a marsh to the east, and an interstate highway to the west. In this situation, the option to expand horizontally is limited by the landscape, the first earth factor. A viable option is to add another level on top of the existing structure. In addition, the existing infrastructure, such as wiring and plumbing (second earth factor), is such that it is less expensive to build up. In the final analysis, the school board accepts a recommendation from the superintendent to add a new floor to the school to meet the needs of the expanding student population.

There are many other stories of modern-day generals in the public education arena. At first glance, they look very much like success stories. However, one must assume a closer vantage point to scrutinize and weigh them by means of Sun Tzu's five factors, which are the triad of heaven, earth, and humanity, flanked by philosophy and method. From this perspective, one can see stories of weak educational administrators, whose main mission is to pacify teachers and thereby avoid the wrath of the union. In an attempt to keep their administrative positions intact, they spoil their troops by letting them take the lead, unchecked and without accountability, neglecting the academic needs of the children. The weight of these phenomena has become so great that our "Nation at Risk" has initiated the No Child Left Behind mandate for all public schools across the nation. Yet it remains an uphill battle to find, implement, and maintain the necessary leadership to foster and ensure adequate (measurable) yearly progress in many of our nation's schools. Educational leadership and accountability is a primary factor in this catastrophe. Strong leaders in the educational arena are rare.

Sun Tzu's sage general leads from a philosophical perspective of being the protector of the state, safeguarding its integrity by defending or conquering. The epitome of a leader represents trustworthiness, knowledge, caring, and courage. He is strict with his troops and with himself. He aligns himself with heaven and earth, with the philosophy of taking the moral high ground. He is the protector of the state. As school leaders, we protect the future of our children. How do we align what is right and best for our children with politics and other factors of the school environment?

BALANCE OF THE FACTORS

It is oversimplifying to present each of the five winning factors as a stand-alone element. The perfect combination of these factors is similar to the yin and yang of Chinese philosophy. In figure 2.2, the outer circle represents the universe, or everything, while the black and white teardrop shapes inside the circle represent the interaction of two energies, called yin (black) and yang (white), causing everything to happen. *Yin* is the dark element; it is passive, dark, feminine, and downward-seeking, and corresponds to the night. *Yang*, on the other hand, is the bright element; it is active, light, masculine, and upward-seeking, and corresponds to the day. Yin is popularly symbolized by water or earth, while yang is symbolized by fire or wind. The right yin yang combination is not completely black or white, just as things in life are not completely black or white. In figure 2.2, embedded inside the teardrop shape is yet another small circle of the opposite, yang and yin. Yin and yang cannot exist independently; they complement each other. They describe two opposite but complementary principles or cosmic forces, said to be found in all nonstatic objects and processes in the universe.

The five winning factors of the *Art of War* can be perceived as having yin and yang states, and the two are in constant movement rather than being held in absolute stasis. An excessive yin or yang state is often viewed

Figure 2.2.   The Yin and Yang Philosophy

as undesirable. The five factors are intertwined, and the various combinations of the factors can produce many permutations, leading to victory or defeat. Mathematically, if each winning factor has a set of yin and yang, then all the five factors can give 2^5 or 32 combinations. As Sun Tzu wrote:

> All five of these factors are critical.
> As a commander, you must pay attention to them.
> Understanding them brings victory.
> Ignoring them means defeat.
>
> (Gagliardi 2003, ch. 1)

A popular Chinese saying reflects the wisdom of the winning factors in the light of the yin and yang philosophy: "The success of a person lies in the harmony that he has with the climate, the ground, and the people." How true that is! When people talk about someone's prosperity in an organization and connect that to the successful interaction of the elements in the organization, they are close to understanding the five winning factors of the *Art of War*.

REFERENCES

Gagliardi, Gary. 2003. *The* Art of War *plus the Ancient Chinese Revealed.* Seattle: Clearbridge Publishing.

The Chronicle of Higher Education. 2006. LIII (6) (September 29).

Hessel, K., and J. Holloway. 2001. *Framework for school leaders: Linking the ISLLC standards to practice.* Princeton, NJ: Educational Testing Service.

3

THE LEADER

THE EMERGENCE OF EDUCATIONAL LEADERS

A number of significant events occurred in the twentieth century that were part of a threat to society and national security in the United States (see figure 3.1). These events bear witness to how the rising tide of mediocrity in education interacted with such national challenges as racial inequality, the space race, and the "War on Poverty." The U.S. government, to better address these threats, enacted laws and set legal precedents affecting the educational rights, entitlements, and responsibilities of all citizens. The results have shaped national philosophy about how the United States educates its citizens to shape the future of the nation. A "war" on these national challenges was declared, and they were "attacked" through the improvement and advancement of education. Every time the country faced a challenge, courageous people stepped up to meet it head on, and leaders emerged.

Attempts have been made to conquer the barriers to progress in this country through education. Unfortunately, these attempts also bear witness to the sheer magnitude of the challenges that remain. In 1892, a landmark decision in *Plessy v. Ferguson* (Tyrack 1967) set the precedent of separate schools for white and black children. This decision held that

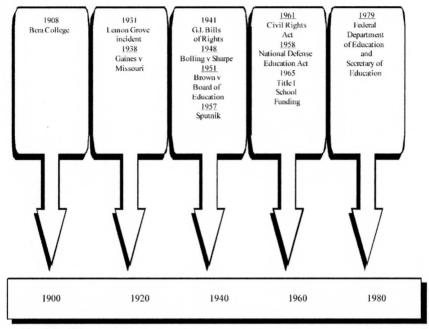

Figure 3.1.   Selected National Events Leading to the Creation of the Federal Department of Education

this division was constitutional as long as the segregated schools provided equal education. Industrialization in the beginning of the twentieth century brought urbanization and ethnic enclaves to cities. Schools in neighborhoods in which poverty prevailed provided poor-quality education. In 1908, the state of Kentucky attacked the racially mixed school of Bera College and mandated separate facilities for black and white students, separated by twenty-five miles. Later, the U.S. Supreme Court upheld this action, in *Bera College v. Commonwealth of Kentucky* (Hall 2005). As a result, Bera College was racially segregated.

In 1931, the tide began to turn. In San Diego, California, Hispanic parents demanded that their children be given the same education as the children of local ranch owners. A judge later ruled in favor of the Hispanic children (Tyrack 1967). In 1938, the U.S. Supreme Court held in *Gaines v. Missouri* (Hall 2005) that the state of Missouri must either allow Mr. Gaines, a black man seeking to enroll in the state law school, to attend, or build him separate facilities. The state of Missouri chose to build separate facilities.

The onset of World War II brought further challenges to the separate but equal doctrine. The armed forces were segregated, with units composed entirely of black soldiers or airmen, as well as entirely Native American, Japanese, or Chinese units. These men often did not receive recognition for their courageous actions during the war; sixty years after the fact, President George W. Bush finally awarded the Congressional Medal of Honor to a black Tuskegee airman, a World War II veteran. In 1944, Congress passed the GI Bill of Rights, guaranteeing veterans access to educational scholarships, home loans, and life and unemployment insurance. The Federal Housing Authority (FHA), which provided low-interest home loans for the postwar housing boom, advocated the use of restrictive covenants to ensure the continuation of segregation in housing developments. However, the Supreme Court ruled this practice unconstitutional in 1948.

In 1950, a judge who ruled in favor of black children in *Bolling v. Sharpe* (Hall 2005) courageously went on record stating that school segregation was humiliating to Negroes, branding them with the mark of inferiority and asserting that they are not fit to associate with white people. The case later went before the Supreme Court, which overturned the decision in favor of the black children.

An important milestone in the advancement toward equality in education in the twentieth century was undoubtedly the landmark case *Brown v. The Board of Education of Topeka, Kansas* (Tyack 1967). The plaintiffs in this case asserted that racial separation in schools, while purporting to provide equal treatment of white and black Americans, actually perpetuated inferior treatment of blacks. Segregation in education varied widely from state to state. *Brown* is undoubtedly the most famous of a series of U.S. Supreme Court cases that dealt primarily with the efforts of racial activists to promote the interests of the people they represented.

In 1951, a class action suit was filed against the Board of Education of Topeka, Kansas, in U.S. District Court. The plaintiffs were Topeka parents, who sued on behalf of their children. The suit called for the school district to reverse its policy of racial segregation. At that time, the Topeka Board of Education permitted school districts to operate segregated elementary school facilities for black and white students. The case began with one concerned parent, Oliver L. Brown, who expressed concern about the "separate but equal" policy of Topeka schools. Brown's daughter, a third grader, had to walk six blocks to her school bus stop to ride to her segregated black school only one mile away. With the encouragement of the National Association for the Advancement of Colored People (NAACP), black parents attempted to enroll their children in the closest neighborhood school in the fall of 1951. They were denied enrollment and directed to the segregated schools.

Linda Brown Thompson, the daughter of Oliver Brown, later recalled her experiences in an integrated neighborhood with friends of different nationalities. She found out one day that she might be able to go to the school that her friends attended, and she was thrilled. She remembered walking over to Sumner school with her father that day and going up the steps of the school. The school looked big to her as a third-grade student. She also remembered going inside the school and her father going into the principal's office, leaving her waiting outside with the secretary. She heard loud voices while her father was in the inner office. Later, her father came out of the office, took her by the hand, and they walked home from the school. Linda Brown Thompson just couldn't understand what was happening, because she was sure that she was going to go to school with all of her friends.

When the class action was filed, Oliver Brown's name was used as a legal strategy to have a man at the head of the roster. The District Court found that segregation in public education had a detrimental effect on Negro children, but it denied relief on the grounds that the Negro and white schools in Topeka were substantially equal with respect to buildings, curricula, transportation, and educational qualifications of teachers. The plaintiffs appealed, and the case went all the way to the U.S. Supreme Court, which decided in favor of Brown in 1954, declaring that separate educational facilities for minorities were inherently unequal. The judges stated that a sense of inferiority negatively affects the motivation of a child to learn. Black children could no longer be deprived of the equal protection of the law under the Fourteenth Amendment. As a result of *Brown v. Board of Education*, the integration of public schools was mandated by the Supreme Court. Not only was this a victory for minority education, it was a victory for minority rights as a whole.

The 1950s marked the inception of an era in which educational controversies came to the forefront in the form of confrontations between students and school and state authorities. The subsequent integration of the educational system heightened racial tensions. In big inner-city neighborhoods, violence and fighting in schools increased. The nation was besieged by protests, rioting, and racial conflicts in almost every sector of society. As a result, the federal government became more aggressive in decision making that effected public education, setting the stage for Congress to pass the Civil Rights Act of 1964 and the Elementary and Secondary Education Act of 1965.

In another arena, in 1957, the Soviet Union successfully launched *Sputnik I*, the world's first man-made satellite. This single event marked the beginning of the space age and the space race between the United States and the Soviet Union. The successful launch caught the attention of the world. It definitely caught the American public off guard, generating fears that the Soviets would be able to launch ballistic missiles carrying nuclear weapons to the United States. Before the United States could even get started with its own satellite launch, the Soviets had successfully launched a second satellite. This time, the craft successfully carried a live dog into space and safely brought it home. Concern over the Soviets' lead in space led directly to Congress passing the National Aeronautics and Space Act, which created the National Aeronautics and Space Administration (NASA) on October 1, 1958, from the National Advisory Committee for Aeronautics (NACA) and other government agencies. In the midst of the Cold War, the United States found itself in a war for possession of the domain beyond the atmosphere of the planet.

Now that the boundaries of the universe were at stake, and the Soviets had taken the lead in space exploration, America was in a great hurry to improve the educational rigor of its schools and the scientific and mathematical skills of its graduates. In 1958, only one year after *Sputnik,* the National Defense Education Act (NDEA) was passed. This legislation provided aid to education in the United States at all levels, public and private, and was instituted primarily to stimulate the advancement of education in science, mathematics, and modern foreign languages. The act also assisted in other areas of education, including technology, geography, English as a Second Language, guidance and counseling, libraries, and educational media. The NDEA provided federal support for improvement and change in elementary and secondary education and capital funding for low-interest loans for students in higher education. As a nation, Americans were fighting hard to win the race for space by beefing up and revamping the educational system. This was becoming a war to stamp out ignorance and to get ahead in cutting edge knowledge, a war that has continued to gain momentum through the present day.

In 1964, President Lyndon Johnson responded to civil rights pressures and religious conflicts over education by linking educational legislation to his "War on Poverty." The Elementary and Secondary Education Act (ESEA) was passed on April 9, 1965 (Kane 1981). This legislation was the most important educational component of the "War on Poverty." It established that children from low-income homes required more educational services than children from affluent homes. As part of ESEA, Title I Funding allocated $1 billion per year to schools with a high concentration of low-income children. This was the beginning of Head Start preschool programming for disadvantaged children. The goal was to obtain equality of opportunity based on the readiness of first-grade children. In addition, Title III services supported Title I through bilingual education opportunities and a variety of guidance and counseling programs. Following the enactment of the bill, President Johnson stated that Congress had taken the most significant step of the twentieth century to provide help to all schoolchildren. He argued that the school bill was wide-reaching because it would offer new hope to many youngsters who needed attention before they even enrolled in the first grade and would help numerous poor families overcome their greatest barrier to progress: poverty. The nation's War on Poverty evolved into a war on our poor and inadequate public education system.

The U.S. Department of Education was established in 1979. Traditionally, the U.S. cabinet has been composed of the most senior appointed officers of the executive branch of the federal government of the United States. Its existence dates back to the first American president, George Washington, who appointed a cabinet of four people to advise and assist him in his duties. Cabinet members are nominated by the president and then presented to the U.S. Senate for confirmation. The approved candidate, after being sworn in, receives the title of "secretary." Until 1979, there was one secretary of health, education, and welfare.

This position combined the three functions in the same department. However, because of the many national challenges and the renewed emphasis on education, a new position was created under President Jimmy Carter in 1979. The secretary of education is fourteenth in line for presidential succession.

Wars, and better still winning wars, in Sun Tzu's time were as important as getting a good education is today. Every time the nation has been confronted by crises, it reacted by boosting the standards and the rigor of education. Therefore education must be conceived of as a means, or in Sun Tzu's terminology, a weapon, for fighting. Education is knowledge and skills acquisition, leading to meaningful applications and problem solving. Education is the basis for understanding, defining, and living a quality life and for shaping and achieving a progressive future for the individual and the nation. It is the foundation for philosophies of consciousness to thrive as opposed to simply surviving. Education is the virtual underpinning of the nation, of life itself. Citizens must know this, and as educational leaders we must know it well! The fight goes on and the war continues. As Sun Tzu wrote:

> This is war.
> It is the most important skill in the nation.
> It is the basis of life and death.
> It is the philosophy of survival or destruction.
> You must know it well.
>
> (Gagliardi 2003, ch. 1)

The survival or destruction of a country depends on good education of its citizens, similar to appropriate military action in times of conflict as Sun Tzu described it. It is important that we examine this foundation carefully. The philosophy is built on the basis for beginning or ending the battle; understand it well, and we shall thrive.

Throughout the years of national challenges, many great people have stepped up to lead and give us the vision to change, and those changes have led to improvement. Among these great people are pivotal educational leaders from all walks of life. We examine the making of the leader (school leader) next.

WHAT MAKES A LEADER?

History reveals that great people emerge in times of need to become leaders. There are two critical questions about leaders and leadership. First is, "What is a leader?" The question is straightforward, and many people would answer, "It is a person who runs things, as in any big or small organization." But this is not a complete answer, because a person who runs things is a boss, and unfortunately not every boss is a leader. The bare-bones definition of a leader is someone with followers—true followers.

This definition prompts the second critical question: "What theories explain why leaders attract followers?" One theory states that a person with charisma has a great potential to become a leader because charisma, like leadership, is a mysterious force that some people are just born with. This belief is known as the Great Man Theory. A second theory says that certain traits favor a person becoming a leader. It is easy to understand that a person who is smart, tall, brave, and strong has a better chance to become a leader than a person who is stupid, short, cowardly, and weak. In this view, it all boils down to our genes. Genetics play an important part in the making of a leader. This is called the Trait Theory. Most people are not cut out for leadership, because they avoid conflict. They run from conflict, but leaders have to confront conflicts and deal with them. The next theory is that a leader in one situation can be a loser in another. This theory suggests that leaders emerge in times of conflict and turmoil. Genghis Khan and Napoleon Bonaparte are good examples. The intertribal Mongol wars gave rise to Genghis Khan, and the French Revolution created Napoleon. Here, the situations and context (Sun Tzu's climate and terrain) shaped and supported the activities of the two men to make them powerful world conquerors. However, if these two men were placed in completely different situations, such as modern-day society, they might end up in jail or be executed, like Saddam Hussein. The proponents of this Situational Theory believe that given the right situation, anyone can be a leader. Successful leaders emerge when their style matches the situation. This is by no means a novel idea. Many years ago, the administrators and the teachers' union in a wealthy school district came to an impasse in contract negotiations, resulting in a strike. Both sides refused to give an inch. On the fifth day of the school closing, a nonunion teacher boldly stepped forward as an unofficial arbitrator, calming both sides and convincing them to reopen the schools. Toward the end, this person single-handedly proposed a compromise, and the schools resumed on the seventh day. The teacher was perceived as a hero and a leader speaking and acting on behalf of the schoolchildren. In just a few years, he moved up through the ranks to become the new principal in a neighboring school district.

Closely related to behavioral science are other theories about the interactions with the environment that make a person what he or she is (Gestaltian theory). With the emphasis on interaction, behavioral psychology rests neither with the person alone nor with the environment alone. The essence of Gestaltian thinking can be captured by Lewin's basic formula (Bigge 1964), $B = f(P, E)$, where behavior (B) is the function (f) of the person (P) and his or her environment (E). In this representation the leader and his or her environment are organized in a field in simultaneous interaction and are mutually interdependent. To a Gestaltian psychologist, "field" means the total psychological world in which a person lives at a particular time.

The theories discussed above give us two extremes to explain what makes a leader. Either leaders are born with leadership, or they acquire leadership through learning. There is no consensus about whether leaders are born or made, whether the leadership capacity comes naturally or is learned. For the purposes of this chapter, leaders are defined as falling in between the two extremes. In other words, leaders are born with certain traits, and those traits are enhanced through learning and life experiences (see figure 3.2).

The qualities you are born with will not make you a leader unless they are developed and given the opportunity to be expressed, which is what schools are supposed to do. In essence, leadership is partly innate, but effective leadership is acquired through learning. Let us examine two examples, an institution of postsecondary education and an athlete, to illustrate the definition of leader and leadership.

West Point Military Academy is a top institution in the country for developing leadership. It offers one of the most highly respected, quality educational programs in the nation, ranking with America's Ivy League universities. West Point focuses on developing leaders of character to

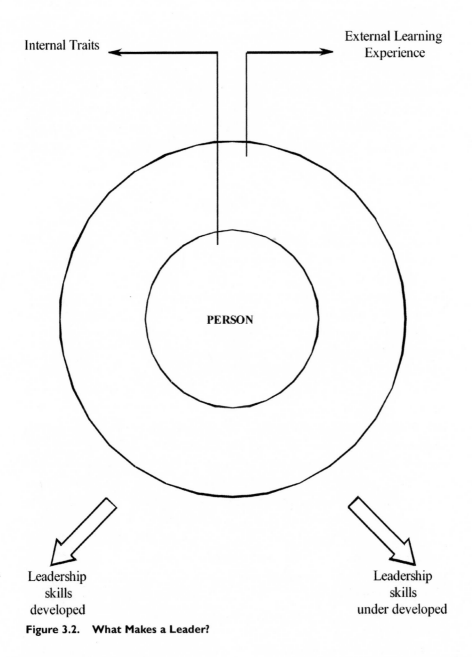

Figure 3.2.   What Makes a Leader?

lead America's sons and daughters in the U.S. Army in times of peace and war. The reward for meeting the West Point challenge is a college degree, a commission as a second lieutenant, and the opportunity to lead soldiers in the world's finest army. A review of its enrollment policy quickly reveals that admission to West Point is a rigorous process. The policy has extremely high academic, physical, and character requirements, and the average admission rate is 14 percent of applicants. Students who apply for admission see a leader inside themselves. They already have the traits of a leader: drive, ambition, and a willingness to sacrifice for goals. However, these traits of students alone do not automatically turn them into leaders. The West Point training gives them the opportunity to express these traits. The institution says, "Give us four years, and we will give you a general." That certainly doesn't happen overnight, but it happens. General Robert E. Lee, General Douglas MacArthur, and General and later President Dwight D. Eisenhower are good examples of how West Point trains people to be leaders.

Who is the recipient of the National Basketball Association's (NBA) Most Valuable Player award five times, an All-NBA First-Team selection ten times, the recipient of the NBA's Final Most Valuable Player award six times, and a member of the Chicago Bulls NBA championship team six times? Michael Jeffrey Jordan. His leaping, or his ability to stay in the air, vividly demonstrated by dunking from the foul line, earned him the nickname "Air Jordan." Michael Jordan is widely accepted as one of the greatest basketball players of all time. Yet in his developmental year as a high school sophomore, Michael was cut from his varsity basketball team because he was considered to be not tall enough. He practiced extremely hard and trained with his coach, eventually earning a basketball scholarship to the University of North Carolina. The legacy of Michael Jordan is a definite interplay between what the man has (his traits) and how he enhanced it through practice and training. Michael Jordan embodies the combination of traits and learning. He is one of the world's most extraordinary physical talents. In spite of his gifts, however, Michael was unable to lead his basketball team to its first NBA title until he learned to help recruit, work with, and collaborate with other key players in a winning team. Over the course of time, Michael learned how to develop his team to its highest abilities, to win the championship. There are two other lessons that we learn from this example: It takes teamwork to win, and part of being a leader is raising team members to levels they would not have been able to achieve on their own. It is significant that Jordan's teammates did not truly excel after they or Jordan left the Chicago Bulls.

What has been gleaned from this review of leadership theories and behavioral psychology theory goes quite well with the wisdom of Sun Tzu, despite the immense gap in time. The broad idea behind the making of a leader is parallel. It is definitely not a coincidence that Lewin's basic formula, for example, bears a close resemblance to the winning factors of Sun Tzu. In table 3.1, behavior in Lewin's formula is compared to the method and discipline of Sun Tzu. The person in Lewin's theory is the leader, and his moral purpose is described by Sun Tzu. Finally, Lewin's environment is heaven and earth.

Obviously, we do not expect Sun Tzu to have used such terms as *traits* and *genetics*; rather, he used internal quality indicator terms, such as *moral purpose, courage,* and *honesty.* The five winning factors are shown in figure 2.1 under internal (the moral law, the commander) and external (climate, ground) categories. Notice that in between the two categories is yet another layer called methods. The method is the interface between the internal quality of the leader and the external environment, commonly known as the *strategy.* Figure 3.2 illustrates the concept of the making of a leader, modified from the original analysis of the five winning factors. The general described in figure 3.2 is bounded by his internal qualities and external strategies. The leadership behavior of a four-star general and a one-star general is driven greatly by each man's internal qualities (i.e., the person) and his interaction with the environment, expressed as external strategies. The four-star general and the one-star general in this example are used to contrast the leadership quality of a high-ranking officer with that of a lower-ranking officer rather than to imply that either has behaved well or badly or wisely or foolishly.

Table 3.1. Comparison of Lewin and Sun Tzu

Lewin	Sun Tzu
Behavior	Method and Discipline
Person	Leader, Philosophy
Environment	Heaven, Earth

INTEGRITY OF LEARNING

> Next is the commander.
> He must be smart, trustworthy, caring, brave and strict.
>
> (Gagliardi 2003, ch. 1)

Scholars of Sun Tzu's work have attempted to rank the leadership qualities he identified, and agree that reliance on intelligence (smart), humaneness (caring), courage (brave), and sternness (strict) separately will result in rebellion, folly, violence, cruelty, and other leadership flaws. For example, exhibiting the leadership qualities of humaneness and strictness in the right proportion will bring the best results in staff management. Practicing the leadership qualities of intelligence and courage in the right proportion will bring the best results in progressive organization planning. Only if we were able to blend all the leadership qualities in a mixer in the appropriate quantities would we be able to create a new, overarching quality of leadership close to the concept of integrity as we understand it today. What is integrity, and why is it important to leadership? A dictionary definition of integrity is, "the state of being complete and undamaged." Unfortunately, integrity is fast vanishing nowadays as leaders are in hot pursuit of shortcuts to success. Leaders are often faced with conflicting desires such as wealth, fame, or power. They struggle to decide between what they need to do and what they want to do. In a situation like this, integrity comes to the rescue and serves as a referee to resolve the conflict. When a person has integrity, what he or she says and does match up, and he or she is trustworthy. A person is who he or she is regardless of time and place, and this is the ultimate standard of leadership. Let us look at a school principal–staff example (table 3.2).

If what the school principal says and what he does are the same, staff behaviors will be predictable. However, if what the school principal says and what he does are not the same, staff behaviors will not be predictable. Many people learn by visual stimulation more than by other senses. So it makes sense that when people see their leader (the school principal) being consistent in what he or she says and does, they believe in that leader.

Table 3.2. Principal–Staff Action Chart

What the Principal Says to the Teacher	What the Principal Does	Staff Behaviors
Come to school on time.	Comes to school on time.	Teachers come on time.
Come to school on time.	Comes to school late.	Some teachers come on time, others do not.

The impact of integrity on leadership is important. First, integrity sets high standards of behavior for the organization. Second, it builds a trusting relationship with followers. Successful leaders maintain high standards for the organization. In the principal–staff example, the principal sets a high standard of coming to school on time all the time. Some people have quite different thoughts about the privileges and the responsibilities of leaders, believing that people high in the leadership hierarchy have more rights and less responsibility. For example, the school principal may come to school on a schedule different from the school's work schedule. However, the greater rights of the leader imply more responsibility, more accountability, and higher standards of behavior (see figure 3.3). A leader who is ready to assume his or her rights, but not so ready to assume his or her responsibilities, will not be around long. A

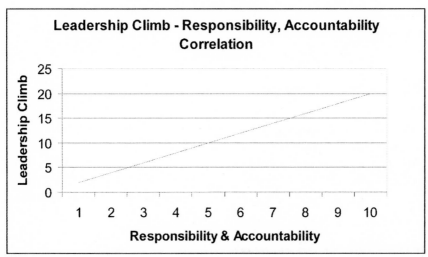

Figure 3.3. Correlation between Leadership Climb and Responsibility/Accountability

leader who has little integrity brings low standards to the organization, and an organization with low standards will not survive.

How does integrity in leadership build trust among followers? To be a leader, one has to have followers. To have followers, a leader must have the confidence to lead. For that reason, an important quality for a leader is unquestionably integrity. If followers find that their leader is not to be trusted, he or she will fail. Authority is not the power a leader has over subordinates, but rather the leader's ability to influence subordinates to recognize and accept that power. Simply put, the leader must build and maintain integrity so that subordinates are able to trust that leader to act in their best interests.

In a Carnegie Mellon survey, only 45 percent of 400 managers believed their senior management, and 35 percent did not trust their immediate supervisors (*CCM Communicator* 1988). With so much at stake, administrators in every organization must lead to improve these less than satisfactory statistics. Without integrity, no real success is possible, regardless of whether the person is a teacher, a department chair, a school principal, a school superintendent, or the president of the board of trustees. A school principal once said: "If my staff understands me, I will get their interest. However, if my staff trusts me, I will get their action." For that school principal to lead, he needs more than a title on his office door. He has to have the trust of his staff so they will follow and support him.

VISION OF LEARNING

Victory comes from knowing when to attack and when to avoid battle.
Victory comes from correctly using both large and small forces.
Victory comes from everyone sharing the same goals.
Victory comes from finding opportunities in problems.
Victory comes from having a capable commander and the government leaving him alone.
You must know these five things.
You then know the theory of victory.

(Gagliardi 2003, ch. 3)

Sun Tzu saw into the future to predict winning or losing a battle. To him, the future announced itself from afar, and he certainly had the experience and the wit to see things before they actually occurred. Historians appropriately call this the "vision of victory." Such vision by itself will not bring victory; it needs support and must be transformed into action.

To be visionary is a fine internal quality that every leader must possess. Vision is defined as the unusual power of imagination to think or plan ahead. Another definition is "something seen in a dream or trance." The ability to imagine and think ahead guides the development and implementation of strategies. Historians fondly cite President John F. Kennedy's announcement that Americans would send a man to the moon within a decade as visionary. The goal was out of this world; nevertheless, it was met. No one doubts that the moon landing was hastened by the vision of this leader and his clear announcement, articulation, and support of the goal.

A few years ago, a group of college visual arts students took a trip to Florence, Italy. The students visited the museum where Michelangelo's famous statue of David is exhibited. As they strolled along the rotunda where this magnificent marble sculpture stands, they also passed a few of Michelangelo's unfinished sculptures. The museum guide explained that Michelangelo literally was able to see images locked in the stone, and it was his task to unleash those images and bring them to life. What the students learned was the ultimate testimony of the power of vision and what it can do to realize the creativity of the artist. The statue of David epitomizes the possibility of the visionary Michelangelo, seeing what others were not able to. In the real work world, a visionary leader can plan long term, see things in a larger context, see through the confusion of a current situation, and determine what is to come.

How do educational leaders build vision? In this era of school accountability, the reform initiative and the standards-based movement must focus on increased academic success for students. The centerpiece of the No Child Left Behind (NCLB) Act makes it very clear that student success matters. This demand for student success has had powerful consequences for teaching practice. It is critical for school leaders to be able to identify and internalize those aspects of administrative

responsibility that promote and support teaching and student achievement. As Gaston Caperton (2001), president of the College Board, stated:

> The principal's influence reaches into every quarter of the school, from
> curriculum and instruction, to order and discipline, to setting an inspi-
> rational and collegial tone for the faculty and staff . . . The school's turn-
> around gives eloquent testimony to the power of excellent leadership
> and strong vision for transforming failing schools into exciting learning
> environments.

The most important question in any organization has to be, "What is
the business of our business?" Answering this question helps to set the
priorities of the organization. In education, without a focus on the
business of the business, a learning organization cannot move forward
and thrive. The Beaumont School District developed the following vision statement to guide its operations: "Beaumont School District 168
is committed to creating a community of life-long learners who will be
responsible citizens in a global and technological society." Here, the vision statement paints a picture of what the school district can become,
showing where the school is heading. For many years, the school used
this vision to guide the collective actions of its stakeholders. To sub-
stantiate the vision of the school district, they also developed a mission
statement to justify the existence of the school: "The mission of the
Beaumont School District 168 is to create and maintain an environment that ensures that every member of the school community reaches
a high level of academic achievement as determined by state and national standards. We commit to a comprehensive system of support to
ensure this outcome."

A new school principal came on board to fill a position vacated by a
veteran leader who retired after twenty years of service. The state of the
Lyons Elementary School could be described as chaotic, with little direction to improve student success despite the fact that the previous
school principal was well liked. The Lyons School Board of Education
hired Ms. Panos to give the school a new vision for improvement. Ms.
Panos had the vision to improve the school; she also understood the importance of developing that vision in collaboration with the school community stakeholders.

Ms. Panos pointed out to the school board that she did not want the vision to stay a vision but wanted to transform it fairly quickly into action. She called together fifty people for a task-oriented meeting. The meeting brought people from all walks of life into the same conversation: How does the school help students to be successful? Attending the meeting were parents, student representatives, teachers, administrators, and citizens. The group met three times in three days to share stories about the school in the past and the present, and about the desired future. Through guided and independent dialogue, people shared and found common ground. Ms. Panos, the mastermind behind the three-day meeting, believed that mutual learning among stakeholders was a catalyst for voluntary action and follow-up. People are more likely to devise new forms of cooperation that continue for months or years if they can settle on a common ground.

On day one of the meeting, people identified key events in the school going back some twenty years, including accomplishments and failures. Small groups shared stories about major events and the implications of their stories for the work they had come to do. Here, the focus of the meeting was on the past. In the afternoon, the group talked about present events affecting them, focusing on the schoolchildren. Much time was spent identifying the impact of the No Child Left Behind Act on the requirements for student attendance, test participation, and meeting the Adequate Yearly Progress (AYP) in reading and mathematics. At the conclusion of the first day, the group had come to grips with the past and the present.

On day two, the stakeholder groups described what they had done about key trends and what they wanted to do in the future. Diverse groups projected themselves into the future and described their preferred future as if it had already been accomplished. The groups posted themes they believed were common ground for everyone in the best interests of the schoolchildren. At the end of the second day, the common ground was confirmed and a new vision was created.

To go beyond the common ground, the newly created vision statement was refined, with the components prioritized on the third and final day. Volunteers immediately signed up to implement action plans. They were sure that there were other options to develop a vision and communicate that to the school community. Through this process, Ms.

Panos allowed the school community to explore the "whole elephant" by visiting the past, the present, and the future that people would like to see. She fostered a meeting climate in which everyone was invited to talk about the same world, the school community. Ms. Panos guided the meeting participants to think globally before acting locally. The school vision was built from the common ground in collaboration with the school community. The vision of Lyons Elementary School was developed to live up to the best in the past and to reach the goals the schoolchildren had yet to achieve.

The vision of a school leader can be assessed in a performance rubric. Hessel and Holloway (2001) developed such a rubric showing four levels of performance indicators: rudimentary, developing, proficient, and accomplished. How would you assess the visionary quality of Ms. Panos and justify the answer with reference to table 3.3.

Table 3.3 defines four levels of performance: basic, developing, proficient, and accomplished. At the basic level, little or no evidence exists for the predetermined behavior. Notice that *basic* does not necessarily mean that the school leader is not capable of the specific set of behaviors found within the category. Rather, the designation simply means that there is little or no evidence of achievement of that component. At

Table 3.3.   The Performance Indicators of a Visionary Leader

| | Level of Performance | | | |
	Basic	Developing	Proficient	Accomplished
A Vision for School Success	There is little or no evidence that the school leader either collects or analyzes data about the school's progress toward the vision.	There is limited evidence that the school leader collects data on the school's progress toward the vision or uses this information to promote student success in any meaningful way.	There is clear evidence that the school leader collects data on the school's progress toward the vision and uses this information to make decisions.	There is clear, convincing, and consistent evidence that the school leader collects and analyzes data on the school's progress toward the vision.

the developing level, there is limited evidence of the behavior. The evidence may not address the component in its complexity, may be lacking in breadth or depth, or may be less effective than expected. For example, the school leader may be aware of the fact that stakeholders should be involved in the decision-making process, but there is only limited evidence that the leader knows when or how to get them involved or is consistent in this fundamental practice over time. At the proficient level, there is clear evidence, which specifically addresses the complexity of the component. In general, the evidence shows that the school leader knows what to do, and does it. At the accomplished level, there is *clear and consistent* evidence. The evidence is very specific and credible. It is comprehensive and thoughtful, presenting an integrated, highly effective approach to the behaviors specified in the component (Hessel and Holloway 2001).

BUILDING AND SUSTAINING A CULTURE OF LEARNING

When was the last time you visited a place outside the country? Did you get a chance to savor the cuisine, talk to the locals, visit the shops, and learn a little bit about the customs? What people do and think is in essence what the culture of a place is about. Conversely, what people do not like and do not value is also a part of that culture. The culture of a place like the one you visited is determined by the people who live there over a long period of time. You do not really have to go far to gain an understanding of the development of culture. Visit a local ethnic neighborhood and you will learn that its culture is what people share in practice, value, and beliefs for many generations.

In education also, what people practice, value, and believe contributes to the culture of the workplace. The positivity of the culture in turn increases the intended achievement of students (Darling-Hammonds 1996). When you work in a school, your behaviors contribute to and shape the culture of that workplace. On the other hand, the culture of a workplace can also influence how you behave. Your contribution to and shaping of a work culture are critical if you are the leader of the organization, because people look to you to model behavior. Leaders in a positive workplace sustain the culture; they need to live up to the culture just like everybody else. Consider yourself lucky if the culture in your workplace is positive and productive. Leaders in a less than positive and productive work culture need to build a new environment and are charged to lead and model that change.

Dr. Lapinski was a high school principal working in a less than collegial work environment. As a leader, he needed to bring about change to improve the work environment. Where could he start? He began with the analysis and assessment of the school culture. He wanted to review a self-study of the school culture before making recommendations for improvement. In collaboration with the school staff, he established five criteria for the school culture self-study: (1) mission and integrity, (2) preparing for the future, (3) student learning and effective teaching, (4) acquisition and application of knowledge, and (5) engagement and service. To further expedite the project, he assigned a committee with six criterion chairs to facilitate the collection and discussion of the information. Dr. Lapinski had the option of administering a forced choice survey to measure the perceptions about the six criteria contributing to the collegial culture of the school. The survey would contain statements describing the criteria and a scale to reflect the respondents' level of agreement with each statement, with a rating scale from strongly agree to strongly disagree (Wong and Lam 2007). However, Dr. Lapinski chose to administer an open-ended opinion poll for each criterion so participants could freely express their ideas without the forced choice limitation.

At the end of six months, the criterion chairs came together to share and summarize their findings. In general, the committee found that the strengths of the school were as follows:

1. The mission (i.e., "The school is responsive to diverse educational needs of the students and is committed to a supportive, lifelong environment empowering members of the school community personally, professionally, and culturally to contribute to a global community.") is the basis for school planning and operation.
2. The school has involved all stakeholders in the shared governance process.
3. The school has been in strong pursuit of external grant funding to sustain, develop, and revitalize academic programs.

4. A new teacher-mentoring program is in place to ensure high quality of teaching and learning in school.
5. The school offers numerous professional development opportunities and recognizes the contributions and accomplishments of staff and faculty.
6. Students receive a wide variety of support (i.e., library, computer labs, academic success center) to help them be successful.

The committee also found that the challenges of the school were as follows:

1. The school is behind in recruiting qualified, diverse faculty members. Currently, the demographic of the faculty is very different from that of the student body.
2. The climate of shared governance has not been reached just by program structures and school board policy.
3. Some of the school facilities are old and maintenance of services are getting to be expensive.
4. The classroom teaching/learning assessment needs to be revitalized to regain its momentum. There is a frequent change of personnel that hinders a continuous process of improvement.

In the spirit of building a climate of collegiality to improve student success, the following recommendations were made and approved by Dr. Lapinski and the board of education:

1. The school needs to develop and implement an effective recruitment plan to strengthen the pool of diverse faculty candidates. This effort could prove difficult because the pool of qualified candidates in the state and the nation is limited, plus the demand is high as many school districts are competing for these excellent candidates.
2. A spirit of shared governance needs to pervade the school, starting from the top and working all the way through the organization. School administrators need to walk the walk of shared governance.
3. The school needs to scrutinize its budget development process to permit the model of money following the students or focusing on

spending money directly to benefit the students. External grant funding needs to be aggressively pursued to secure additional financial support.

4. Policies and guidelines of effective teaching need to be established, and the performance of staff and faculty needs to be assessed against the guidelines.

(The general process of the self-study has been simplified here to focus on the concept of assessing and improving the culture of a school, without burdening the reader with the planning and implementation details.)

> You must learn through planning.
> You must question the situation.
>
> Some commanders perform this analysis.
> If you use these commanders, you will win.
> Keep them.
> Some commanders ignore this analysis.
> If you use these commanders, you will lose.
> Get rid of them.
>
> (Gagliardi 2003, ch. 1)

Sun Tzu advised leaders to educate themselves through the analysis of strengths and challenges (weaknesses) (i.e., the culture) of the organization. Effective leaders build on the strengths and work on the challenges, and Sun Tzu would advise being patient about the process. Changing school culture is about changing people's deepseated behaviors in the face of their resistance to change. It takes more time and effort to change attitudes than to change knowledge and skills. Many people feel that changing culture is destabilizing. For that reason, it is not difficult to understand why many people are not ready to embrace change.

The National Policy Board for Educational Administration states that an important duty of the school administrator is to promote positive school culture. To achieve this, the school administrator must assess school culture using multiple methods and implement context-appropriate strategies that capitalize on the diversity (e.g., population, language, disability, gender, race, socioeconomic) of the school community to improve school programs and culture. The policy also states that the administrator must develop a sustained approach to improving and maintaining a positive district culture for learning that capitalizes on multiple aspects of diversity to meet the learning needs of all students.

MANAGING AN ENVIRONMENT OF LEARNING

> Use a cup of the enemy's food.
> It is worth twenty of your own.
> Win a bushel of the enemy's feed.
> It is worth twenty of your own.
>
> (Gagliardi 2003, ch. 2)

> All successful armies require thousands of men.
> They invade and march thousands of miles.
> Whole families are destroyed.
> Other families must be heavily taxed.
> Every day, a large amount of money must be spent.
> Internal and external events force people to move.
> They are unable to work while on the road.
> They are unable to find and hold useful jobs.
> This affects seventy thousands of families.
>
> (Gagliardi 2003, ch. 13)

Sun Tzu explained that a major military campaign was a severe drain on the nation's resources, including people, labor productivity, and finance. He realized that resources must be allocated to the right places to survive in a competitive environment. Sun Tzu employed quantitative accountability to insinuate the creativity and productivity of a resource manager. In "Going to War," Sun Tzu offered suggestions to minimize costs by feeding off the enemy. In "Using Spies," Sun Tzu suggested the prudent management of resources. In these two examples, Sun Tzu pointed out the interchangeable skills of a manager and a leader. In other words, elements of management can be a part of leadership, and vice versa.

Some years ago, the state of Illinois worked more aggressively toward improving schools and students. Among the many improvement initiatives was the definition of an *instructional leader*. A question raised about the definitive role of school leadership was, "How much time should the school principal spend in the lunchroom, the playground, the classroom, and the office?" An attempt to answer the question prompted a survey of the school principals of a large suburban comprehensive school district. To the surprise of many, the survey revealed that principals spend more than half of their workday in the office dealing with paperwork, projects, and other mundane chores. Aren't school principals supposed to be the leaders of teaching and learning? How can they be effective instructional leaders if more time is spent in the office than in the classroom? After much research and debate, the state finally came up with a simple requirement that the instructional leader spend at least 50 percent of his time in the classroom. Are you an instructional leader of your organization? Do you know how much time you spend where teaching and learning need you most, the classroom?

Student learning is considered to be the heart and soul of education. It is measured by the No Child Left Behind Act against a predetermined achievement standard. Learning obviously does not happen in a vacuum. No one will argue that learning requires effective teaching first and foremost. For that matter, schools are paying greater attention to ensure that resources are meticulously managed to support learning and teaching. The following accounts relate how the school budget is managed in Woodfield School District to support learning and teaching, how staffing is managed in Mohawk College to support a student-centered environment, and how personnel and budget are grossly mismanaged in Minolta School.

Mr. Casing is a retired school business manager in Woodfield, a comprehensive K–12 school system. He gave an account of how the school budget was prepared and managed to support the district's mission of effective programs that lead to academic excellence (i.e., successful learning) for all students. Mr. Casing did not work in isolation. Instead, he involved the stakeholders in the school community: citizens, the school board, the superintendent, staff, and teachers. The process involved a cause-and-effect process that was activity based. The correlation between the money spent (input) and the intended performance (output) measured the effectiveness of budget preparation and management. In an ideal world, a small input (i.e., resources) would generate a large outcome, which in education to a large extent is student achievement. Another way to explain this process is to justify why the money is being spent to achieve certain objectives, thus linking resources directly to student performance.

Let us analyze the activity-based budget (ABB) process (figure 3.4) to better understand the skills of school resource management. In contrast to the traditional method of budget management, done mainly by the business manager and his or her staff, ABB is open, collaborative, and constructive. The purpose of the process is to allocate financial resources using broad stakeholder input and involvement in the budgeting process to help guide the future direction of the school district. This is accomplished through the support of effective programs that lead to academic excellence for all students.

Activity-based budgeting starts in September to prepare the school budget for the following year. In Woodfield, the business manager invited a group of citizens in the community to a series of advisory committee meetings. These citizens were local business experts who gave

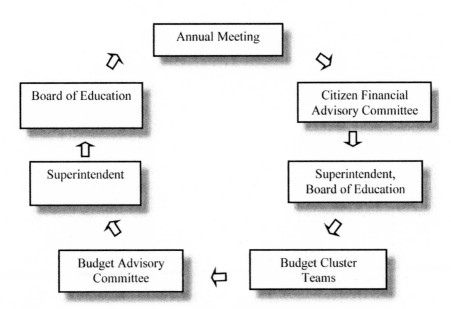

Figure 3.4. The Activity-Based Budget (ABB) Cycle

advice on financial matters. The committee defined budget parameters for the upcoming school year based on the resources available. The recommendation was then presented to the board of education in mid-October. The recommendation was later forwarded to nine cluster teams for fine tuning. The cluster teams represented the major operations of the schools: the high school cluster, the middle school cluster, the elementary school cluster, the building and grounds cluster, the technology support cluster, the media support cluster, the athletic cluster, and the learning support cluster. Each cluster reviewed the budget allocation for its specific operation. For example, under the learning support cluster were the salaries of the administrators, the staff, instructional equipment, acquisition of printed materials, communication, and publicity. The main budget items under learning support are summarized:

Administrator	$ 107,209
Staffing	$ 917,740
Instruction	$ 127,299
Equipment	$ 239,954
Printed materials	$ 323,249
Communication	$ 62,545
Total	$1,777,996

Budget preparation at the cluster level was crucial because the team maintained, increased, or reduced the budget items. Each cluster team was given the charge of preparing four budgets. Level I was a plan with a 10-percent budget reduction. Level II was a budget with a 5-percent reduction. Level III was a plan with no reduction. Finally, Level IV was a budget with a 5-percent budget increase. Obviously the Level II budget, with the greatest reduction, was the most challenging to prepare because the team had to come up with a justification for budgetary changes while maintaining the operation and support for the main operational objectives of the school district. If Mr. Casing could ask Sun Tzu for advice, he would tell Mr. Casing to put the resources where they are most needed. Definitely, the Level-II budget should be the most revealing in terms of shaving the extras. The four levels of the learning support budget are summarized:

Level I	10% decrease	$1,600,179.30
Level II	5% decrease	$1,689,078.20
Level III	status quo	$1,777,996.00
Level IV	5% increase	$1,866,875.80

The process was concluded in February, when the business manager called all the teams together for the cluster budget presentation. It took three evenings to accommodate all the presentations. Each was carefully and constructively discussed, and at the conclusion all stakeholders voted and ranked the priority of all the budget proposals. Their recommendation was presented to the superintendent and the school board to finalize and to ensure that the budget was both safe and legal. Finally, at the annual meeting at the end of the school year, the electorate at its public hearing meeting approved the budget and the tax levy.

In ABB, the final approved budget (the product) and the process of preparation are equally important. In many budgeting processes, only the top administrators are privileged to make decisions. In this case, Mr. Casing used broad-based input to make important budgetary decisions about the effective management of learning resources. This process exemplifies effective management of resources in the ideal world of shared governance of an organization.

Mohawk is a two-year community college serving a diverse student population. The Adult Education Department is funded by the government and the college to assist adults in becoming literate, in obtaining the educational skills necessary to become full partners in their children's education, in completing their secondary school education (by passing the General Education Development, GED, examination), and in obtaining the knowledge and skills necessary for employment and self-sufficiency. It is envisioned that coordination of the adult education services will facilitate the elimination of the barriers facing individuals with low literacy skills who are seeking training and employment. To that end, the Adult Education Department offers four main lines of instructional services to assist students in transitioning to postsecondary education, vocational training programs, and jobs (see figure 3.5).

The services are access to literacy, English as a Second Language (ESL), General Education Development (GED), and High School Credit (HSC). Student success does not stop with the completion of

STUDENTS

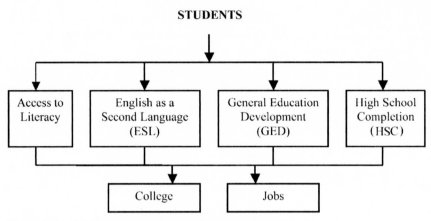

Figure 3.5. Adult Education Instructional Services

these programs. Students need to continuously transition to pursue a college degree, obtain a job, or improve in a job. How should the department be staffed to deliver its services? This is a human resources management challenge. In developing the staffing plan, several criteria were used. (1) First and foremost, the system is student centered. The dean of the department explains this effectively: "The success of the student is top priority. It is like the celestial sphere on the shoulders of Atlas (i.e., the support of the faculty and staff) in Greek mythology." (2) The four lines of instruction have to be connected to facilitate the transition of services. (3) Classified staff members are cross-trained to support the entire department. When the organizational chart (see figure 3.6) was presented, many people thought that the design was upside down, with the students on top and the chief administrator of the department at the bottom. One can easily see that staff placed at the very top side of the chart have more direct contact with students. They are the instructors and student workers. As we move down the chart, people at the assistant director and technical support levels are less directly working with students. Finally, staff at the director and dean levels are purely supportive to students.

Mohawk Community College also has a large science department serving some 6,000 students. The department has two science cochairs, Ms. Honson and Mrs. Murphy, due to large student enrollment. Ms. Honson engages herself in hiring, training, and scheduling em-

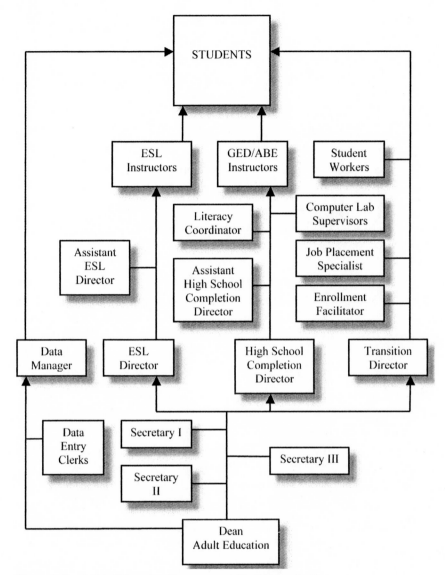

Figure 3.6. Adult Education Department Staff Organization

ployees to accomplish work in the most efficient and effective manner possible. Three years ago, Ms. Honson was charged to hire new staff for the growing science department. She undertook the project with enthusiasm. She hired faculty members who could competently work the assignment, would accept the modest pay, and had expertise in teaching in science. Ms. Honson measured her success by efficiency and cost effectiveness. However, Ms. Honson did not anticipate that of the faculty members she hired, only a handful would still be working there one year later. Mrs. Murphy, the other science co-chair, received the same assignment as Ms. Honson. Mrs. Murphy hired faculty that she believed she could develop a working relationship with, rather than hiring those who would work the assignment and take the modest pay. Mrs. Murphy's goal was to hire a diverse group of faculty members, some even fresh out of college, with whom she felt she could develop a personal connection. A large part of Mrs. Murphy's training involved team building, sharing success stories, and listening to faculty to improve the department. Mrs. Murphy also measured success in terms of efficiency and cost-effectiveness, but in addition, she measured success in terms of low staff turnover and high morale.

What is the major difference in leadership roles between Ms. Honson and Mrs. Murphy? Who is the manager, and who is the leader? Can a leader be a manager and a manager be a leader? The answer is "absolutely." The skills of a leader and a manager are not mutually exclusive. A leader who only exhibits leadership skills will be ineffective when it comes to checking time schedules, approving requests to attend professional development conferences, and scheduling employee vacation time, things that employers require their managers to do on a timely basis. Similarly, a manager who spends all his or her time completing paperwork and reading reports only creates more problems for himself or herself because he or she lacks a developing relationship with employees. If you are a manager who has spent too much time managing and not leading your employees, start spending more time leading, until you can firmly establish your time in leadership practices. If you are a leader who only likes to lead, either become a politician; hire an assistant to be your manager; or start spending at least half of your time getting the paperwork done, taking phone messages, and answering e-mails.

> Some leaders are generous but cannot use their men.
> They love their men but cannot command them.
> Their men are unruly and disorganized.
> Their soldiers are useless.
>
> (Gagliardi 2003, ch. 10)

According to Sun Tzu, some leaders may compensate people well but not value people. These managers may care about individuals, but they do not guide them, causing them to be confused and not feel valued. Staff under such mismanagement are useless, as Sun Tzu concludes about soldiers. There are no hard-and-fast rules for personnel management because it is like picking the right temperature porridge for Goldilocks, not too hot and yet not too cold.

The following account from Minolta School illustrates challenges in budget and personnel management. Upon accepting a position as principal of a new school, a woman was told by her predecessor, "You will love it here. The teachers are wonderful here; you couldn't ask for a better group of teachers. They know their jobs well and they know just what to do. You couldn't ask for more." Upon meeting the teaching staff, the new principal was repeatedly informed that the former leader always supplied teachers with blank checks to purchase supplies before school started. The former principal had allocated $2,000 per teacher for school supplies, plus an additional $1,000 to use for personal development at their discretion, and another $500 for any additional needs that teachers felt might arise during the course of the school year. This all sounded very abundant and encouraging to the new leader. However, when attending to the budget, she discovered that there was also an abundance of money set aside in separate categories to address all the same needs that teachers were now spending "their money" on. Many supplies had already been ordered from this budget, and many teachers were demanding to keep "their" full $2,000 budget intact. In spending the separate $2,000 teacher budgets, most teachers purchased items many educators would consider nonessentials, such as numerous prizes for children, candy, three times the needed number of crayons per student, colored paper, pencil boxes, the most expensive folders, student backpacks, etc. All this seemed questionable, and when the budget was examined further, it showed that total teacher expenditures on nonspecific items and capital of "their choice" exceeded $150,000. Total money allocated specifically for textbooks and curriculum was a mere $17,000.

The former principal had assumed that teachers best knew the needs of their students. The new principal had a difficult time turning the situation around, because the teachers loved their former leader, who had lavished money on them to spend at their discretion, with little accountability for improved student achievement. Most teachers were unaware of specific curriculum objectives, and there was no unified, strategic plan in place to indicate the direction of many core areas of study, including behavior plans for students. This was why many teachers were heavily engaged in frivolous spending on student-pleaser gifts and sundries for the students. Students were being spoiled by the teachers. The teachers continued to demand their "right" to former money allocations and processes. The road to new thinking about how to specifically address the needs of students based on raising student achievement, and in keeping with all educators being held accountable for developing educational strategies and methodologies for improving student achievement, was a very difficult one for a new commander in charge of spoiled soldiers.

To lead or to manage is the choice facing many administrators. What does it mean to be a leader and what does it mean to be a manager? Is being a leader different from being a manager, and is it possible to lead and manage at the same time? Are you a leader or a manager? Are you some of both or all one or the other? Are you an Albert Einstein? He was extremely knowledgeable but much more interested in the ways things worked (a characteristic of a manager) than in what the theory of relativity could do for humankind. Or perhaps you are an Abraham Lincoln. He was extremely frustrated by events around him and willing to step forward and make sacrifices to change the status quo (a characteristic of a leader). Both are important. Imagine what the world would be like without Einstein or Lincoln.

PARTNERING WITH THE SCHOOL COMMUNITY TO FOSTER LEARNING

> Manage your government correctly at the start of a war.
> Close your borders and tear up passports.
> Block the passage of envoys.
> Encourage politicians at headquarters to stay out of it.
> You must use any means to put an end to politics.
>
> (Gagliardi 2003, ch. 11)

For a school leader to be effective, he or she needs an environment that supports his or her vision to foster learning. A department chair of a school defines the environment as the staff and faculty of the department. A school principal defines the parent–teacher association as his environment. A superintendent of a school district reaches out to the larger school community to define her environment of support. Here we have a broad spectrum of the school leader's environment, from a department of a school to the community boundaries of the school district. Regardless of the size and complexity of the environment, the school leader works with people to make group decisions, and the process of making such group decisions involves politics. Politics in its simplest form applies to all human group interactions, including educational institutions. In a broader sense, any human group interactions involving a power struggle or maneuvering for power can be described as politics. When the school leader makes decisions in collaboration with school community constituents with different priorities and power relations, the school leader works with politics, and sometimes dirty politics.

A veteran school principal of an alternative education center laments that her many years of professional training did not prepare her well to be a politician in education. She spends most of her time dealing with people, building relationships and steering people in the organization in the right direction. She admits that theory learned in the university graduate course on educational leadership is one thing, and how it works with real people is yet another. The school principal advises aspiring administrators to stay out of school administration if they do not enjoy working with people or do not like to deal with politics.

Another school superintendent helps us to understand how he works with people and deals with politics in a different and more successful way. This school administrator works in the same large alternative education center as the previous veteran school principal. He understands the significance of sharing his vision and seeks support from the school community as education partners. Where should he begin this mammoth task of building educational partnership? He worked closely with the parent–teacher association (PTA) in his previous principal position, and he thought about using a similar PTA concept in his new job, planning to expand and refine it to become the School District Planning Council

(SDPC). With the vision to lead in partnership with the school community, the school superintendent charged the SDPC to develop and coordinate educational programs in the school community to serve its diverse population, who are not enrolled or required to be enrolled in secondary school under the state law. These transient students are characterized by a lack of sufficient mastery of basic educational skills for functioning effectively in society; do not have a secondary school diploma or its equivalency; or are unable to proficiently speak, read, or write the English language. SDPC membership includes government entities, and related community representatives are strongly invited to participate.

In his inaugural SDPC meeting, the school superintendent made it clear that shared governance and accountability go hand in hand. This concept was new to many members, and it took the council almost the entire first semester to understand. The alternative education center continuously used student data to define the success of the school operation. The data included gains in student education, student retention rate, and student transition to postsecondary education rate as measures of program success. In other words, the program was not successful until the students were successful.

Two years after the establishment of the SDPC, the program had grown rapidly in increased student enrollment and student work placement. People did not see the impact of the school–community partnership until they saw employees of local employers returning to school to finish their high school equivalency diplomas or improve their English language proficiency! Furthermore, the transient population created a continuous replacement of workers in many local businesses. Where could these employers find workers quickly to keep the business going? These employers had connected with the job placement office of the alternative education center and had been successful in placing students in jobs that they had prepared for.

At the commencement ceremony of the alternative education center, a former graduate of the center, then a division manager of a local manufacturer, thanked the center for preparing him for the real work world and thanked the manufacturer for giving him an employment opportunity. The school superintendent commented after the presentation that the student was the epitome of student success through school–community partnership.

REFERENCES

Bigge, L. M. 1964. *Learning theories for teachers*. New York: Harper & Row.

Caperton, Gaston. 2001, May. What America's leaders are saying about the principalship. *The College Board News*. In *NewsLeader* 49 (6) (September 2001): 1.

Darling-Hammonds, L. 1996. The quiet revolution: Rethinking teacher development. *Educational Leadership* 53 (6): 4–10.

Elmore, R. 2000. *Building a new structure for school leadership*. Washington, DC: Albert Shanker Institute.

Gagliardi Gary. 2003. *The* Art of War *plus the Ancient Chinese Revealed*. Clearbridge Publishing.

Hall, Kermit L. 2005. *The Oxford companion to the Supreme Court of the United States*. 2nd ed. Oxford University Press.

Hessel, K., and J. Holloway. 2001. *Framework for school leaders: Linking the ISLLC standards to practice*. Princeton, NJ: Educational Testing Service.

Kane, Joseph Nathan. 1981. *Facts about the presidents*. 4th ed. New York: H. W. Wilson.

Tyrack, David B. 1967. Turning points in American educational history. New York: Blaisdell.

Wong, Ovid K., and Lam Ming-Long. 2007. *Using data analysis to improve student learning, toward 100% proficiency*. Lanham, MD: Rowman & Littlefield.

④

WAGING WAR

As previously defined, *war* and *enemy*, in the application of Sun Tzu's strategy in education, are really about solving (i.e., fighting) problems (i.e., the enemy) to improve schools and student success rather than fighting people who hate and harm you. In this chapter, Sun Tzu's strategies for waging war are used to shed light on tackling challenges and solving problems in education.

The *Art of War* is all about winning with strategy, not war. The strategy applies well to a wide range of human activities, including success in education, business, career, and even challenges in one's personal life. In addition, strategy is a process that is embedded in a comprehensive plan. Sun Tzu replaced the focus of fighting with the concept of advancing one's position against the opponent. Most of Sun Tzu's work explains what is entailed in mastering these skills of advancing positions in a competitive environment:

> Some field positions are unobstructed.
> Some field positions are entangling.
> Some field positions are supporting.
> Some field positions are constricted.

instead of moving in and attacking. Why? The answer is found in the *Art of War*, chapter 3, where Sun Tzu wrote that the best way to win a battle is not to fire a shot but to make the enemy surrender (i.e., foil the enemy's plan). In the rules of making war, Sun Tzu offered a spectrum of strategies, from surrounding, to attacking, to defending, to evading the enemy. In essence, there are three basic strategies a leader can take: seeking positions, attacking, and defending (see figure 4.1).

When the reflective leader is not certain of a sure victory, he or she is in the mode of strengthening resources or finding the way until he or she can attain a winning position. In the competitive business world, to find a winning position can mean the use of deceptive moves and manipulation to achieve a goal. When the insightful leader is confident about the strength of his army, he attacks. When the perceptive leader assesses the strength of his army to be weak, he digs in his heels to defend. The connections among the three basic strategies are fluid and interchangeable. Many leaders feel that the offensive and defensive modes of operation are mutually exclusive. In the continuous growth of an organization, it is possible to integrate offensive and defensive oper-

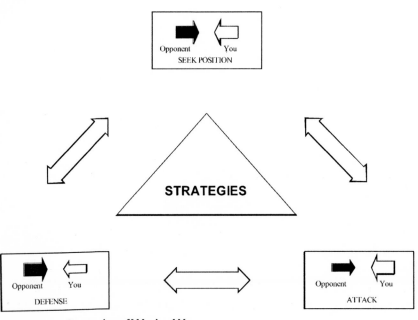

Figure 4.1.   Strategies of Waging War

> Some field positions give you a barricade.
> Some field positions are spread out.
>
> (Gagliardi 2003, ch. 10)

Sun Tzu's classical strategy consists of analyzing one's position and the methods for moving to new and strategically advantageous positions in preparation for victory. Sun Tzu wrote that the analysis of one's own position is always relative. When we say that the position is unobstructed, we are in fact saying that the position is open with reference to the enemy. If Sun Tzu's army is on high ground, he is in an advantageous, unobstructed position to view the enemy. On the other hand, if the enemy is on high ground and leaves, then the enemy loses the unobstructed field position. Sun Tzu would advise a general to entice the enemy to leave the high ground and strike him as he is leaving, to gain what is called the "supporting field position." When Sun Tzu wrote, "Know yourself and know your enemy" in chapter 3 of the *Art of War,* he was in fact advising assessing one's position in relation to that of the enemy. As a leader one must understand the situations and the factors that create the positions, the advantages, and the disadvantages. As a leader, one must also understand and know how to deal with different positions regardless of whether the army is gaining or losing ground.

THE STRATEGIES OF WAGING WAR

> The rules for making war are:
> If you outnumber enemy forces ten to one, surround them.
> If you outnumber them five to one, attack them.
> If you outnumber them two to one, divide them.
> If you are equal, then find an advantageous battle.
> If you are fewer, defend against them.
> If you are much weaker, evade them.
>
> (Gagliardi 2003, ch. 3)

Sun Tzu's guidance for making war is unique in that even if his army outnumbers the enemy force ten to one, he would surround the enemy

ations. Every organization or program must go through a continuous cycle of creating, preserving, assessing, and changing. Creating and changing are offensive functions. Preserving and assessing are defensive functions. When an organization is continuously on the offensive, it will consume a lot of resources, with little reflection and improvement. On the other hand, if an organization is continuously on the defensive, it will not reach any new heights of achievement. Combining the two is similar to attaining the yin and yang equilibrium of the environment. Finally, the leader executes his or her orders and keeps in mind the influence of the five winning factors: philosophy, climate, ground, leadership, and military methods (as described in chapter 2).

SEEKING POSITIONS

Creating a winning war is like balancing a coin of gold against a coin of silver. Creating a losing war is like balancing a coin of silver against a coin of gold.

(Gagliardi 2003, ch. 4)

See the time to move.
Don't try to find something clever.
Hear the clap of thunder.
Don't try to hear something subtle.

(Gagliardi 2003, ch. 4)

Sun Tzu's idea of positioning means moving to a new position only when an opportunity presents itself clearly, like a clap of thunder, instead of fantasizing about subtle improvements that are not even there. Sun Tzu further taught that a winning campaign must be aimed at an *opening*, what we would call a *window of opportunity*.

How will the strategy of seeking positions apply in the classroom and in a school organization? Let us study a forward-looking classroom teacher preparing herself to be a school administrator. Ms. Hernandez was a position to prepare to achieve her goal of moving up the career ladder and find an administrative post in the school organization. She fully understood that she had to be ready when an administrative opportunity became available. She explained to her staff later that she had to prepare herself for when opportunity knocked on the door. She understood that student success was goal number one for the school and that the level of school achievement was determined by the annual mandatory state examination results. For a number of years, Ms. Hernandez worked diligently, coaching her class for the state examination while at the same time being very active in leading her grade level colleagues in curriculum and student assessment development.

One year, the school principal announced his retirement, and in that same year Ms. Hernandez achieved a high score in her class state examination report. Was the opportunity for advancement presenting itself like a clap of thunder? You bet. She proved herself to be an instructional leader by bringing her class, first and foremost, to a high score in the state examination, and by her additional administrative experience in leading her grade level in various important school projects.

Sun Tzu counseled leaders to wait patiently for the appropriate opportunity (i.e., seek positions). He taught that we cannot create opportunities most of the time, but we have to be ready when an opportunity presents itself. In other words, when the opportunity calls for the gold coin to outbalance the silver coin, the leader must seize the chance to advance.

Tom and Doug are two independent educational consultants for Fennville, an established publisher of school textbooks. The two men service the northern and southern regions of their state respectively, covering numerous school districts. Every year, they make their rounds, visiting schools to market new textbooks. Tom seeks positions to break into the school market. He pays attention to the state published school report card, the budgetary allocation of student resources for the individual schools, and the state text adoption cycle. Doug, on the other hand, pays attention to the alignment between the publisher's text and the state learning standards, the ancillary materials for teachers, and pricing. Tom and Doug are both top consultants, but who is in a better position to be an outstanding sales consultant in the long run? Let us analyze the tools (see table 4.1) that Tom and Doug use as they seek the winning position to break into the school market for textbooks.

With reference to waging war, who are the opponents? Are they the school people that Tom and Doug deal with? Sun Tzu wrote in the *Art of War*, chapter 4, that "Winning a battle is always a matter of people.

Table 4.1. Information Tools

Tool	Information That the Tool Brings
1. School report card	The school report card, which contains vital school information, is officially published annually by the state department of education. The information includes student demographics, attendance, graduation, budget, and disaggregated student achievement data, as well as proposals for improvement. The report card also shows the improvement status of the school.
2. School budgetary allocation	The school budget is open information and is frequently reported in public school board meetings. Undoubtedly, the bulk of the budget is spent on personnel. Per student budget allocation is important. It shows the budget spent on teachers, services, and supporting materials, such as textbooks. Is the budget about the same as the state average? Is it more? Or is it less?
3. Learning standards alignment	Learning standards are what drive the development of curriculum and student assessment development. The standards are content specific, and the mandatory state examination is based on assessing what students know and what they can do with reference to the standards. Many rules and regulations from the No Child Left Behind Act are based on student achievement of learning standards.
4. State text adoption cycle	Individual states have a schedule for text adoption. The schedule describes a rotation of state funding support by subject matter (math, reading, science, social sciences, etc.) and by grade levels (K–12), on a five- or seven-year cycle. For example, a certain year is the year for elementary science adoption, and funds are allocated by the size of the school or school district. Many schools align the adoption of their textbooks with the schedule of the state adoption to defray the costs of text purchase.
5. Ancillary materials	Ancillary materials are important supporting materials for the main program. These resource materials could be in the form of student workbooks, posters, transparencies, student assessment, and other student and teacher materials. If adopting a text program is in the hands of teachers, ancillary materials can be a big deciding factor, as many teachers would not want to tackle the textbook with little support.

. . . This is a matter of positioning." Or are the opponents the publishers competing to win in the market? How would you advise Tom and Doug to meet the unserved market, and what tools would you advise them to use to win victory? Is it possible for Tom and Doug to see a window of opportunity, or is it possible for them to create one?

In seeking winning positions, the leader needs to make calculated decisions. Whether to attack or to defend is a question a leader frequently

asks when seeking positions. Eventually, the decision will lead him or
her to victory or defeat. Sun Tzu's wisdom in making calculated decisions is data based, pure and simple:

> This is the Art of War:
> Discuss the distances.
> Discuss your numbers.
> Discuss your calculations.
> Discuss your decisions.
> Discuss victory.
> The ground determines the distance.
> The distance determines your numbers.
> Your numbers determine your calculations.
> Your calculations determine your decisions.
> Your decisions determine your victory.
>
>   (Gagliardi 2003 ch. 4)

Simplistically, in Sun Tzu's time the decision was based on a calcula-
tion of numbers that gave the leader information critical to ground wars.
Using quantitative data to improve student learning is not new to education. In the wake of the No Child Left Behind Act, schools are measured by the non-negotiable quantitative evidence of student success.

One task that many school administrators are familiar with is developing a semester class schedule, based on student enrollment and a host of
other factors. Let us visit Mr. Riley and Mrs. Kim. They are two assistant
high school principals in the same town. Well before the beginning of
the school semester, the assistant principals have to make decisions, individually as well as collaboratively, about course schedule development.
Such decisions are made based on student enrollment data, teacher
availability, time availability, and classroom space availability, all put
together in a rather sophisticated document called the semester class
schedule. A foremost deciding factor for a class is student enrollment:
"Do we have enough students to run the class?" From a business point
of view, it is not cost effective to run a class with just a handful of students. Schools normally adhere to the class enrollment policy as described in the teachers' contract. Class enrollment is considered an important work condition for the teachers. For example, the school

administration may not force a teacher to teach a class with thirty-five students. In addition, certain special education classes have a lower teacher–student ratio, to maximize learning success. For laboratory courses, such as advanced placement (AP) chemistry or physics, the class may be limited to twenty students because the laboratory can only seat that many. A high student–teacher ratio reduces student–teacher interaction and attention given to individual students and thus diminishes the quality of learning. Under extreme conditions, the teacher can get additional compensation for teaching a class over the student enrollment limit. When the assistant principal prepares the semester class schedule, he or she is constantly calculating factors to seek the position of pulling the perfect schedule together. Mr. Riley ran into a challenge one semester as the preparation of a semester class schedule was underway. He saw seven students on the list for AP chemistry, and that number would definitely not make a class. He picked up the phone and called Mrs. Kim right across town to inquire about her AP chemistry student recruitment. Mrs. Kim had a similar challenge of low student enrollment for AP chemistry. She had eight students. What were their options? Mr. Riley and Mrs. Kim could either cancel the class because of low student enrollment or combine the students from the two schools to make a class. What is the best decision in the best interest of the students?

Collaboratively, the two assistant principals combined the students and located the class in Mrs. Kim's school, because hers was new, with better laboratory support. The teamwork of Mr. Riley and Mrs. Kim is what Sun Tzu described as finding the opportunities hidden in common problem situations. He mentioned in chapter 7 that "problems can become opportunities."

> You make war using a deceptive position.
> If you use deception, then you can move.
> Using deception, you can upset the enemy and change the situation.
>
> (Gagliardi 2003, ch. 7)

The leader might have to make deceptive moves to gain a position. In war, for example, a deceptive retreat of an army might lure the enemy to advance and fall into a trap. A well-known example is from the Greek siege of Troy, which lasted ten years. The Greek devised a deception, a giant, hollow wooden horse filled with Greek warriors. The rest of the Greek army appeared to retreat. Meanwhile, a Greek spy convinced the Trojans that the horse was a gift. Eventually the Trojans accepted the gift and brought it into the city because it was customary for a defeated general to surrender his horse to the victorious general as a sign of respect. The Trojans celebrated the end of the siege, and when the Greeks emerged from the horse, the city was in a drunken daze. The Greek warriors then opened the city gate to allow the rest of the army to enter, and Troy was finally taken. The term *Trojan horse* is now used to describe an apparently advantageous position that is actually a trap in disguise. Trojan horse strategies are sneaky, underhanded, and deceitful.

War historians cite the defeat of Napoleon in the decisive battle of Waterloo as an example of victory using military strength and deceptive warfare strategies. The Duke of Wellington, the commander in chief of the allied troops against Napoleon, was able to conceal the strength of his army by hiding it behind the landscape.

Another well-known example of deception in warfare is recorded in Chinese history, about 800 years after Sun Tzu. There was a major military conflict between the Han dynasty and another neighboring state. Kung Ming (*Kung* literally means an opening, and *Ming* means light; the name means an opening with light) was the witty and most supreme counsel of Han. It was recorded that toward the end of the Han dynasty, Kung Ming's imperial city was surrounded by a huge army led by General Ssu-ma Yee from the opposing state. Early one morning, General Ssu-ma's army was at the city gate getting ready to storm the city. General Ssu-ma hesitated to order the attack because he knew Kung Ming's reputation for shrewdness. While Ssu-ma's soldiers were standing by to attack, the city gate slowly opened, and out came several peasants. These peasants did not pay much attention to the surrounding enemy soldiers but went about their business of sweeping and cleaning the city gate entrance, while Kung Ming sat comfortably watching and smiling from the top of the city gate. The standoff did not last long, and finally General Ssu-ma ordered a retreat. What happened, and who won? Kung Ming won, and he did not even move a single soldier. He used the supreme strategy of deception, which Sun Tzu would have approved. Remember that the ultimate strategy of the *Art of War* is to win without fighting. During the standoff General Ssu-ma made the assumption that the open city was actually a trap. This "empty city strategy," ingeniously concocted by Kung Ming, is still used today to gain an advantageous position.

Which of these three examples of deceptive warfare would Sun Tzu cite as the ultimate example? Undoubtedly, Kung Ming's victory over General Ssu-ma Yee would be his choice, because the battle was won without fighting, and not even a single drop of blood was shed.

The use of deception is very common in military conflicts, because its application may bring victory and save lives. Deception is accepted in the military because no right or wrong is used to judge its application. It is the final defeat or victory that matters. But how far can we go in using deception in education? Deception is interpreted as wrongful and unethical, bringing about harm and damage. Deception in education is clearly not desirable, and it is considered unacceptable because it does not support the philosophy of ethics and values of teaching. If education supports deception, we are also saying that we support dishonesty and other unprofessional behaviors. It is unfortunate that "if you can get away with it, it is okay" tends to be the moral principle of the day. For example, surveys indicate that 75 percent of high school students have admitted to cheating on tests (Bracey 2005), and cheating appears to be on the rise throughout the grade levels (Goodman 2005; Selingo 2004). The American public is increasingly looking to educational institutions for solutions to problems such as these.

Let us study an example of deception and its consequences for the individual and the school. A big city school was in the news because the principal was charged with accessing classified information online. The news reporter later revealed that the charge against the school principal was actually made by the school superintendent. A few days later, the news reported that the board of education wanted to discharge the school superintendent because the superintendent had illegally accessed the school principal's computer. The final decision about the case was pending for an extended period of time while it was argued who was at fault for being deceitful and unethical. The questions were, "Was the principal guilty? Or was the superintendent guilty? Or were they both guilty?" It was obvious to the public that the two top school administrators had attempted to move into a position for personal gain at the expense of the integrity of the profession and of the students.

Two teachers are in conversation about their work at school. One teacher says, "Teaching is what I do every day. I am entitled to all my sick days, personal days, and other benefits that go with this job." The other teacher says, "I am getting paid to help kids learn. If kids do not learn, I am not earning my paycheck." The two teachers are obviously different in their points of view about teaching. The second teacher relates her work to what is professional and ethical. To view teaching as just another job is simply deceptive and unprofessional, and does a disservice to our students, parents, and the community.

Schools are governed by the code of ethics of the education profession. There are two principles under the codes of ethics published by the National Education Association (NEA). The first is "commitment to the student." The second is "commitment to the profession." The school principal and the superintendent discussed previously violated the principle of making a professional commitment to the student by disclosing information obtained in the course of professional services not required by law or for a compelling professional purpose.

Let us study another example of professional deception, falsification of professional competency. A candidate applied for an entry-level administrative position in a large school district that required a bachelor's degree. His resume showed that the candidate had a professional doctoral degree from outside the United States. He had also taken courses in a master's program. The impression given to the search committee was that the candidate had professional qualifications. On closer examination of his credentials, it was found that the foreign doctoral degree had no equivalency in the United States. Furthermore, although he had taken courses in a master's program, he did not have a master's degree.

One can read about cases of deception in the media every day. Such behaviors bring both shame and penalty to the person and the organization. Outside schools, corporate scandals lead to the collapse of businesses such as Enron and WorldCom, and deceptive accounting practices have brought shame to the business community and American society in general. Accurately weighing strengths and weaknesses to seek an advantageous position is preferred, and the use of deceit and dishonesty should never, ever be considered.

ATTACKING

> Attack when you have a surplus of strength. . . .
> Move your forces when you have a clear advantage.
>
> (Gagliardi 2003, ch. 4)

> You win in battle by getting the opportunity to attack.
>
> (Gagliardi 2003, ch. 12)

Sun Tzu advised giving the order to charge if one has the strength and the opportunity. When one has a surplus of strength (i.e., soldiers and resource), as a leader one is ready to make the move to attack. What is strength, and what is opportunity? In education, strength can mean knowledge and skills required by the profession. When someone has acquired knowledge and skills, that person is ready when opportunity knocks on the door.

A young education student was once asked by his professor about the acquisition of knowledge and skills needed to prepare him to be a teacher. The novice student quickly responded by equating knowledge to taking courses and working toward a professional certificate and a degree program. Skills, he said, were a bit more difficult to master, because he had to transfer the book knowledge to classroom applications, and sometimes there is no obvious direct transfer. An example would be management of the school lunchroom and the playground, because there were no specific theories and guidelines to do lunchroom and playground management. The student concluded that when he attained 100 percent of the knowledge and 100 percent of the skills as certified by the state board of education, then he would be ready to be a teacher and tackle the real world. The old professor smiled and asked the student to think about the following. There are twenty-six letters from A to Z, and if each of the letters is represented by a number from 1 to 26, then A is 1, B is 2 . . ., and Z is 26 (see table 4.2).

Assuming that a point in the table is the same as a percent, what percentage of being ready for work does KNOWLEDGE represent, according to the alphabet-point table? Knowledge gets 96 points, or 96 percent (K = 11, N = 14, O = 15, W = 23, L = 12, E = 5, D = 4,

Table 4.2. Alphabet-Point Table

A	B	C	D	E	F	G	H	I	J	K	L	M
1	2	3	4	5	6	7	8	9	10	11	12	13
N	O	P	Q	R	S	T	U	V	W	X	Y	Z
14	15	16	17	18	19	20	21	22	23	24	25	26

G = 7, E = 5). What percentage of being ready for work do SKILLS represent, according to the alphabet-point table? Skills get 82 points, or 82 percent (S = 19, K = 11, I = 9, L = 12, L = 12, 2 = 19). If knowledge gets 96 percent and skills get 82 percent then what gets 100 percent? is the answer is attitude. ATTITUDE gets 100 points or 100 percent (A = 1, T = 20, T = 20, I = 9, T = 20, U = 21, D = 4, E = 5, total = 100). Many veteran teachers agree that knowledge is what they teach on a daily basis, and skills are applications of knowledge. It is attitude, not knowledge or skills, that is the most challenging to attain. It might take years of experience to adjust, and many more years to groom the right attitude for work and for life. In essence, knowledge, skills, and attitude are all important ingredients of success. Interestingly, knowledge alone or skills alone will not get a person 100-percent ready. In other words, attitude is everything! Attitude is the foundation, and it needs to be broad based and deeply rooted.

A study of many highly successful leaders, such as Albert Einstein, Helen Keller, Winston Churchill, Mahatma Gandhi, and Franklin D. Roosevelt, reveals that they had handicaps. Some were born in poverty; others came from broken homes and were placed in difficult or challenging environments. Why did they achieve and overcome problems, while many others stumbled? The answer is attitude. These leaders refused to yield to obstacles and turned their stumbling blocks around to make stepping stones. These leaders also realized that they could not control their circumstances but could determine their attitude toward those circumstances.

DEFENDING

Defending is preserving one's current position with insufficient strength or resources. Defense does not go after new positions, and it is less costly and risky than attack. When a person is on the defensive it may be because he or she is being attacked. Will a problem attack people (task related), or will people attack people (people related)? It is obvious that when someone is being attacked, whether it is task related or people related, the attack will still ultimately be people driven. Problems and issues continually occur at work and in life, and if tackling problems is like fighting battles, then we are faced with different forms of fighting every day. Some battles are fought over task problems, and others are fought over people problems.

An irate school principal asked one of his department chairpersons to visit his office and raised a concern about the decline in projected student enrollment for the following new school semester. This was a task problem (student enrollment projection); however, it was driven by the school principal (people). How should the department chairperson have responded to being "attacked"? What the chairperson did was respectfully ask the principal to validate his data; it turned out that he had mistakenly used the wrong data to project student enrollment. What we learn from this strategy is to defend with data verification. Data are facts. Without data support, any statements, claims, decisions, or accusations will just be the opinion of yet another person. As a school leader, one can turn the same strategy around and use data verification to render the person involved defenseless. A school psychologist had a habit of leaving work early. The principal gave him a verbal warning and a posted note to remind him to adhere to the office work schedule. When the behavior did not change, the principal wrote the school psychologist up, with an accurate documentation of all the dates on which he had left early. The school psychologist was not able to defend against data verification because it speaks louder than opinions.

Another form of defense is called *defensiveness*. When people are being defensive they may be covering up mistakes, may be giving excuses, or may feel insecure. In the real work world, many people are defensive about what they do or how they behave, especially when they get into trouble. In education, we see this often in the classroom. We also see it, although hopefully less often, in the school board room. Teachers are all too familiar with what students say when homework is not turned in on time or is missing. "I was not feeling well," or "The dog tore up my homework" are common student words of defense. Often, these are not defenses but rather excuses.

When school leaders are habitually defensive, they are in fact not stepping up to responsibility. Sometimes leaders themselves resist change. If a leader has created a program that is being phased out for improvement, he or she might see the change as a personal attack and will respond defensively. A social worker visited a state penitentiary and discussed with the inmates why they were in prison. Typical responses were, "It was not me but somebody else"; "I was framed"; "It was mistaken identity"; etc. The social worker wondered if anyone could find such a large group of "innocent" people anywhere else but in prison. School leaders need to take charge and step up to responsibility and accountability, to stop being defensive or making excuses. When we take complete responsibility for ourselves, when we stop making excuses, we start to move to or stay at the top.

Figure 4.2 reminds us that leaders cannot evade responsibility. When workers in an organization get into trouble, the leader also gets into trouble, no matter what the excuses are. If a worker in an organization goofed, and he or she was not qualified to do the job, then it was the leader's fault. If a worker goofed and did not get sufficient support in the organization, then it was the leader's fault again. Can we simply say that the mistake did not occur? If a leader says that nothing happened, he or she is being dishonest, and it will be his or her fault again the next time something goes wrong. Simply stated, leadership comes with accountability, and evading accountability will simply not work.

A progressive leader is always in the mode to seek advantageous positions to advance and make gains for the organization. This mode of operation is fluid, in that the leader sometimes has to retreat and at other times has to move forward. Sun Tzu would advise the leader to "wage war" based on a good understanding of the winning factor involved.

REFERENCES

Bracey, G. 2005. A nation of cheats. *Phi Delta Kappan* 86 (8): 637.

Gagliardi, Gary. 2003. *The* Art of War *plus the Ancient Chinese Revealed.* New York: Clearbridge.

Goodman, J. F. 2005. How bad is cheating? *Education Week* 24 (16): 32, 35.

Selingo, J. 2004. The cheating culture. *Prism* 14 (1): 24–30

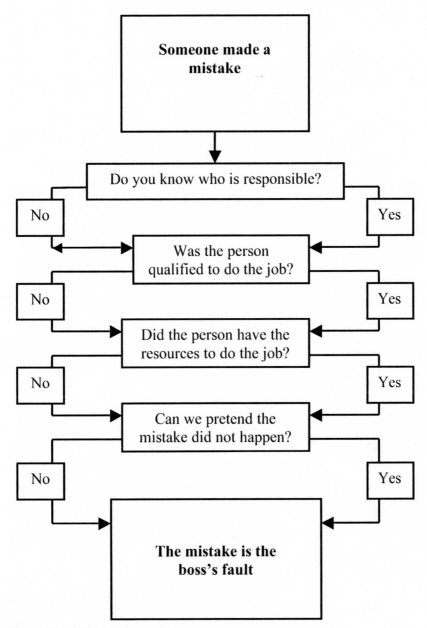

Figure 4.2.   Who Is Responsible?

5

COMMUNICATION

You can speak, but you will not be heard.
You must use gongs and drums.
You cannot really see your forces just by looking.
You must use banners and flags.
You must master gongs, drums, banners, and flags.
In night battles, you must use numerous fires and drums.
In day battles, you must use many banners and flags.
You must position your people to control what they see and hear.

(Gagliardi 2003, ch. 7)

In Sun Tzu's time, the maneuvering of an army in the battlefield was a challenge because of the limitations of communication and the immense number of soldiers. A visit to the terra cotta warrior museum in Xian (see figure 5.1), China, will give you an idea of what the commander of the ancient army was up against. The life-sized terra cotta warriors, with their chariots and horses, are arrayed in an impressive battle formation much larger than a football field. At the eastern end of the formation are three rows of vanguards, all armed with bows and arrows. The wooden parts of the original weapons, of course, long ago disintegrated through

Figure 5.1.   Terra Cotta Warriors, Xian, China

time and the elements of the earth. Immediately behind the vanguards is the main body of the battle formation. There are horse chariots with armored soldiers holding weapons like spears and halberds. Around the outer edge of the formation is one row of archers with crossbows facing north, south, and west to protect the flanks and the rear of the army. It is estimated that more than 6,000 terra cotta warriors and horses will be unearthed from this spectacular archaeological dig. To win the battle, a commander needed to effectively communicate and maneuver his massive army against the enemy.

In a similar vein, the school leader needs to communicate with his or her constituents about the safe and effective operations of classrooms, schools, and the school community, so students will learn and be successful. In the tasks of school leadership, communication between leaders and constituents goes beyond the obvious and conscious levels to envisioning goals, affirming values, motivating and managing, achieving unity, renewing, and last but not least, teaching. Sun Tzu wrote that armies should use different means, such as banners, flags, gongs, and drums to communicate. In other words, amplify different ways to reach and control what constituents hear and see to ensure good communication.

Like the commanders of the ancient armies, school leaders nowadays need to communicate effectively with people in the organization to be successful, and there are no exceptions. All of us must communicate with superiors, coworkers, and subordinates to be effective in what we do. In the school environment, we work internally with the board of education, the superintendent, central office administrators, school principals, teachers, paraprofessionals, and other support staff. Externally, we need to communicate with parents and other community members who need or provide services to the schools. If we are like other people in the workplace, the biggest challenge we face is less the knowledge that we need for the job than communication with other people. The ability to get a message across clearly, diplomatically, and assertively affects our success more than any other skill. Adding power communication to one's skill repertoire will raise and assure one's leadership profile in the school organization.

The success of a school leader depends on relationships, and relationships depend on good communication. Good communication depends on clear purposes, paying careful attention to the message, and thorough awareness of the audience. The goal of this chapter is to suggest ideas for clear and effective communication to make the relationships between the leader and his or her organization more harmonious. As a school leader, you can greatly enhance your organization's success by improving your own communication skills.

WHAT IS COMMUNICATION?

Listening, speaking, reading, and writing are ways to communicate to reach mutual understanding. Communication involves at least two parties, a sender and a receiver. The sender is the person expressing the message to others. The receiver, on the other hand, is the person who gets the message from the sender. In good communication, the sender sends the message and the receiver receives the message, and they each take turns being the sender and the receiver. When a party in the process dominates being the sender or the receiver, communication falters, and tension builds up like a tug-of-war.

The goal of communication is to share information and reach mutual understanding. When this goal is achieved, participants in the process understand each other. Have you seen how two lumberjacks work with a saw to cut down a tree? The logger on each end pushes and pulls the saw in harmony; as one pulls the other pushes, and vice versa. The saw does not work to achieve its function if the loggers both push or both pull at the same time. Seeing how two lumberjacks work with a saw is similar to seeing two people collaborate to communicate.

What about disagreements? Disagreements are fine as long as the process is sincere and respectful. Differences are issues to be worked out by the communicating parties to reach the desired outcome. To reach mutual understanding requires deliberate efforts that are not aggressive, not selective, not passive, but rather assertive, attentive, and active.

What are the "Ways of Communication"? In the school environment there are different ways to communicate, much like the gongs, drums, banners, and flags of war in Sun Tzu's time. There are the chain of command, meetings, presentations, memos, writing, and simply making decisions in the hectic life of a school leader. A major difference among the communication categories is the level of formality and complexity. One tends to think of the chain of command, meetings, and presentations as formal, and memos and conversation as informal. In formal communications, participants expect to resolve problems and make decisions. In addition, what happened in a formal meeting is also expected to be recorded as minutes and reports. In the less formal categories of communication, people expect more information sharing, with less decision making. As a pivotal school leader, one has to master a certain level of proficiency in all categories of communication.

CHAIN OF COMMAND AS A FORM OF COMMUNICATION

> You control a large group the same as you control a few.
> You just divide their ranks correctly.
> You fight a large army the same as you fight a small one.
> You only need the right position and communication.
>
> (Gagliardi 2003, ch. 5)

Communication is at the heart of the leader–follower relationship. The larger the organization, the greater will be its complexity, and the more challenging will be the two-way communication necessary for effective functioning. The best school leaders recognize that even if a free flow of communication is practiced, those at other levels will filter, analyze, interpret, condense, and distort the original message. In this excerpt, Sun Tzu explained that the size of an organization does not change the rule of communication. The leader communicates clearly to a small group of people the same way he or she communicates clearly to a large group of people: by focusing on getting an advantageous position, establishing clear lines of communication, and communicating effectively.

People in the field of education are familiar with the chain of command of a school organization. At the top is the board of education, followed by the superintendent, then the school principal(s), then the teacher(s), and then the students. When a problem, such as student management or achievement occurs, the first person to respond is the classroom teacher. If the problem cannot be resolved by the teacher, the problem goes up the chain of command to the school administrators. The chain of command is often perceived as a linear management series in order of authority. When the chain is followed properly, the flow of communication is distributed and regulated. This section describes a different configuration of command that is more like a two-dimensional web than a linear chain.

Many school emergency situations are handled locally. In the case of a major incident, however, help may be needed from other area jurisdictions. The Eagleton School District has three comprehensive K–8 districts: Beaverton, Oakton, and Morton. The combined student population of the three districts is more than 10,000. People in the community felt that a straight chain of command in emergency situations might not be effective because of the large size of the three districts combined. In 2006, all the administrators of Eagleton were invited to a planning meeting to discuss how they could work cohesively to respond to natural disasters and emergencies, including acts of terrorism. The purpose of the planning committee is to develop unified guidelines for incident management and standard command and management structures, with emphasis on preparedness and resource management. It was agreed after days of deliberation that clear lines of communication had to be established and published. Administrators at all levels are required to complete mandatory training using the guidelines. In addition, successful completion of the training includes passing an online examination. Such communication lines enable constituents to understand clearly where the decisions and orders are coming from and where they are going without being hindered by jurisdictional boundaries. The planning committee agreed on establishing six units of communication: the primary execution of command functions; the collection, evaluation, and dissemination of tactical information; the provision of facilities, services, and materials; the monitoring and assessment of hazardous situations; the inventory of resources committed to the incident; and the dissemination of information to the public. All the units are headed by a team of administrators representative of the larger Eagleton area. One challenge of the planning committee was to connect the units in such a way that they could respond immediately and effectively to an incident as a group. The planning committee came up with a web, with the incident command post as the brains of communication. The connections of the command post to the other units are shown in the Eagleton Incident Communication System (figure 5.2).

Early one Friday morning, as a drill, an urgent message came to the office of the superintendent that the Eagleton school community had an unusual pattern of absenteeism. The message simply stated that a large number of students and employees had not reported to schools. In addition, a number of people on campus felt sick. The superintendent and the administrative team immediately met and activated the functions of the command post. First and foremost, and according to the previously established guidelines, no one was to give any order or do anything until they had heard from the central command. In a matter of minutes, directives were given to the operation unit to barricade all traffic going to and from schools. Directives were also given to direct all people who felt sick to go to the school gymnasium, where they were to be made comfortable and given any necessary attention. To do that, the resource unit and the logistic unit were asked to assist. The team in charge of the safety unit was told to monitor the campus to curb activities that might pose hazards to public health. Calls were made to the neighboring hospitals to

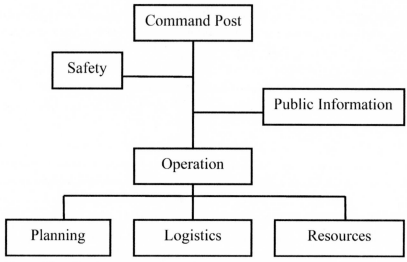

Figure 5.2. The Eagleton Incident Communication System

find out if there were similar reports of outbreaks. The public information unit was directed to hold information for radio or television inquiry until they heard from the command post.

In a less than two hours everyone in the Eagleton school community knew exactly what to do. It was reported later that the incident was a drill and that Eagleton had passed the test of what to do in case of an emergency. Eagleton is a large school district, but the rule of communication is accurate and consistent. Thanks to the establishment and application of the web of command, the people of Eagleton are ready to tackle real-world emergencies.

MEETINGS AS A FORM OF COMMUNICATION

Meetings are held frequently in the life of a school leader. Because of the increasing prevalence of shared governance and decision making, effective meetings have become more important than ever. Two-way communication, as in meetings, is essential to proper functioning of the leader–follower relationship. There must be easy and proper communication from leaders to followers, as well as adequate return communication. Meetings in essence are face-to-face communications. Nothing can substitute for a live person listening attentively and responding to another person. In a meeting, there is more to face-to-face interaction than purposeful speaking and listening. The leader's behaviors carry messages and demonstrate that messages are received. For building trust, loyalty, and motivation, electronic messages are far from adequate.

Put yourself in the shoes of a teacher. How many meetings are you supposed to attend? Now, put yourself in the shoes of a school administrator or a school district administrator. How many meetings are you supposed to attend? You will find that there is a direct correlation between the number of meetings that you must attend and your position or level in the school organization. As you rise in the organization, you can be certain you will attend more meetings. As a school leader, you will find your schedule filled with your fair share of meetings with the board, the supervisors, coworkers, subordinates, students, and other members of the school community. Meetings are inevitable in the life of a school leader. It is important that they be planned and executed effectively. Figure 5.3 shows the decision to have a meeting and the details that follow that decision.

What do school leaders need to accomplish in meetings? Can they accomplish the same goal if a meeting is not held? A crucial question the school leader needs to ask before a meeting is whether the meeting is necessary. What are the other communication options, such as memos or phone calls? As a school leader, do you feel that you are calling too

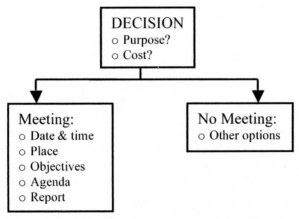

Figure 5.3. The Many Decisions about a Meeting

many meetings, with their purpose not well defined? Do you call a meeting because you want to give people the impression that you are doing something, to deal with the interests of a few people in the organization, or just because this is a routine of the organization? A meeting called for any of these reasons might not be well defined or even justified. The school leader should be prepared to answer an audience member who asks, "Why did you call this meeting?"

From the business point of view, meetings can be translated into measurable expenditure because they draw on resources like time and personnel. Is the meeting more cost, or more benefit? Shouldn't the school leader decide more carefully about meetings if they are costly, just as he or she decides whether to buy a new computer for the school? Do you know how expensive a meeting is? Add up the per-hour salary of each person at the meeting and the portion of their benefits (about 14 percent of the salary). In addition, consider the lost productivity of the participants. In other words, what would those people be doing or working on if they were not attending the meeting? Unnecessary meetings can be a loss of the organization's productivity. Other measurable meeting expenses may include utilities, refreshment if provided, and depreciation of equipment. Aside from the obvious tangible meeting costs, other intangible costs could end up being even more expensive. Consider how people may complain about bad or unnecessary meetings and how that negativity can affect the morale of the organization. The negative impact of staff's low morale is not measurable but does have a cost. Let us visit two schools to examine the measurable and immeasurable impacts of a special curriculum project.

A new mandate in the state learning standards has prompted schools to make changes and adjustments to those learning standards. Triton and Morton are two schools in the same suburb of a large metropolitan city. They spend the same amount of money per student, indicating a similar community support for education. The principal of Triton School and the principal of Morton School planned a series of curriculum committee meetings, knowing well that the alignment of the state curriculum to classroom instruction and eventually the student state test performance would be greatly affected. The questions that faced the two principals were how many meetings should be called, how many teachers should be involved, and how many resources should be mobilized.

Knowing the important purpose of the meetings, the principals knew that they were beyond answering the initial question of meeting or not meeting. The Triton principal hired a curriculum consultant from the university and asked the consultant to lead and facilitate a group of grade-level teachers in developing a new standard-based curriculum in the fall semester. The plan was to pilot the new curriculum in the spring semester, discuss the findings with the board curriculum committee, and present the final recommendations to the superintendent and the board of education. The budget estimate for the Triton curriculum project from start to finish was $8,500. The Morton principal, on the other hand, purchased cutting-edge software and charged her to develop the standard-based curriculum. She consulted a university professor to refine and finalize the curriculum before presenting it to the superintendent and the board of education. The Morton curriculum project cost $7,600.

As a school leader, would you choose the Triton project or the Morton project of curriculum development? Is your choice based on the cost or on other factors? One would select the Morton project if cost were the only consideration. However, what good is an inexpensive project if it does not bring victory or results through the ownership and unity of staff? In the scenario, the Triton project cost more, but it was staff driven, a bottom-up model of curriculum development. The Morton project cost less and was for the most part technology driven, a top-down model of curriculum development. In the *Art of War*, Sun Tzu used communication to unite the army:

> You must master gongs, drums, banners, and flags.
> Place people as a single unit where they can all see and hear.
> You must unite them as one.
> Then the brave cannot advance alone.
> The fearful cannot withdraw alone.
> You must force them to act as a group.

> (Gagliardi 2003, ch. 7)

In this excerpt, Sun Tzu stated the ultimate goal of strategic communication: to unite different groups into one. In times of confrontation and challenge, unity is strength.

Now that you have decided to call a meeting, you need to prepare for it. The preparation involves giving people notice beforehand about the purpose and agenda of the meeting. Without information, the participants might come unprepared with issues and ideas. For that reason, the meeting leader must let people know ahead of time the date, the time, the location, the purpose, the agenda, the expected outcome, and what people need to bring or prepare. You could do this formally or informally, perhaps sending out a written agenda ahead of time. If you are attending a meeting, ask what you need to prepare, because every person at the meeting is responsible for making the meeting a success. Table 5.1 is an example of a meeting agenda.

You might need to pay attention to the room arrangements if you want the meeting to be effective. Long boardroom tables can create a very formal atmosphere, giving people a feeling of "us versus them." A horseshoe or circular seating arrangement can provide more face-to-face interaction. A classroom seating arrangement might give people the feel-

Table 5.1.   Meeting Agenda

Washington Academy Staff Meeting		
Meeting called by: Phone:		
Meeting participants:		
Meeting date: Meeting time: Meeting place:		
Topic	Person Responsible	Time
(1)		
(2)		
(3)		
(4)		
(5)		
Etc.		

ing of a teacher and student configuration. Regardless of the room arrangement, it should give participants a sense of occasion and purpose.

How do you get the most out of a large meeting, and what is the process of communication? In a large meeting, the normal protocol is to have only one person speak at a time. This format is fine; however, it will limit the discussion of multiple topics. How then can we conduct a large meeting to deal with multiple topics? First, decide on the categories of information that you need to collect, such as opinions, concerns, or needs. Second, divide the group into as many small groups as there are categories of information. Three to five people is a good small group. Assign each group the task of collecting information, and give it a reasonable amount of time to do that. At the end of the meeting, allow each group to present its findings orally or using visual support such as a transparency or flipchart paper. Some might want to put the flipcharts up on the wall for additional group discussion. Dividing a large group into small teams is a good way to inject energy into a meeting, to have some fun, and to get things accomplished.

How do leaders behave in a meeting? To be the superintendent, the principal, or the department chair does not make a person a leader. Just because someone is given the power to run a meeting does not necessarily mean that person is a meeting leader. True leadership is earned, not given. Have you attended a meeting without leaders? People just go round and round in endless and off-track discussions. On the other hand, have you attended a meeting where only a few people are engaged and the rest just listen passively, with little or no participation? A good leader will not allow either situation to occur; he or she is prepared. The leader does his or her homework on the issues to be discussed and gives an informed and objective point of view appropriately. The point of view often comes in handy to break a tie in a heated discussion. A leader may also solicit the viewpoints of participants early on in a discussion because he or she often the one making the final decision.

The leader is expected to make contributions in a meeting. This does not necessarily mean lengthy discussion, but can be brief, frequent, and relevant comments. The comments can be quick suggestions for directing or changing the course of a discussion, such as "What do you think?"; "Let's get back on track."; "Good idea, I like that . . . "; "What you are saying is . . . "; "Let's see who is going to do what and when." These quick comments are attempts to request input, get the meeting back on track, encourage contributions, summarize, or draw a discussion to some meaningful conclusion, and translate that into an action plan. One good way to finish a meeting is to give each participant an opportunity to express a last thought, make a last comment, or have the last word. These closing thoughts and comments can ensure full participation, reduce unstated agendas, and most of all, summarize the meeting. We do not expect people to open up new agendas and extend the meeting. For that reason, ask everybody to contribute and limit each individual's time to one minute. As the leader, insist that comments be heard with respect and appreciation.

Finally, nonverbal communication is also very important. A good leader is expected to use a clear, inflected voice, appropriate body gestures, good eye contact, and effective facial expressions. You might want to observe the meeting behaviors of leaders in your next meeting and record their effectiveness. Learn from the good behaviors and avoid the ineffective ones to reflect and improve your own skills in meeting leadership.

After the meeting, people expect to get a summary of what was decided, supported by pertinent discussions. The strategies to accomplish this are very straightforward. Avoid off-track "he says and she says" types of information. Keep the information concise and accurate to promote understanding and retention. Focus on major decisions and action items. Table 5.2 is a template for meeting minutes. At the top, the minutes include a record of who attended the meeting. A list of who was not at the meeting is probably not necessary, and might embarrass those who did not attend, creating animosity. It is more appropriate to talk with the non-attendants privately and firmly if the behavior is habitual. In the left-hand column are the major topics as listed in the original meeting agenda. To the right is a record of what was discussed, including action items and the individual(s) responsible for follow-through. Many organizations have the luxury of having a recording secretary for taking minutes. It is also common for meeting participants to take turns being the recording secretary. This creates an atmosphere of shared rather than passive participation.

The epitome of all meetings is the school board of education meeting, or simply the board meeting. Board meetings are dreaded by many

Table 5.2. Meeting Minutes

Washington School Staff Meeting (Date of Meeting)			
Attendance:			
Guests: (if applicable)			
Meeting called to order: (time)			
Topic(s)	Discussion	Action	Responsible Individual
(1) (2) (3) (4) (5) Etc.			
Adjournment: (time)			
Respectfully submitted by:			
(name of meeting secretary)			

school leaders because of the level of formality and exposure to the public. In such formal meetings, important decisions are made by the elected board officials on a regular monthly or biweekly schedule. In general, the agenda of a board meeting has three major components: the consensus agenda, department or committee reports, and citizen hearings.

First and foremost are the consensus items. The consensus agenda contains a number of decision items that the board approves or disapproves. Such items can include budgetary, personnel, and contractual matters. It is customary for the board not to discuss personnel issues in an open meeting. Rather, they retire to discuss personnel issues in closed sessions. In the consensus agenda, board members exercise their power to pass or not pass the items. One reason for the board to make such crucial decisions on the spot is information that they received prior to the meeting. Such prior information is normally distributed in an information package called the board packet. The packet is sent to the individual board members days before the meeting. In other words, board members are informed before the meeting.

Next are the department and committee reports. Department and committee reports are presented to share school initiatives and project information related mostly to school operations and student achievement. As a presenter you can be sure to invite board questions if this meeting is the very first time they hear about something you are presenting. An ideal situation is to keep a board member serving on the board subcommittee informed in prior board subcommittee meetings. Let the subcommittee comment and ask difficult questions to their heart's content. What you present to the board subcommittee meeting in this case is simply a dress rehearsal for the real board meeting.

Last are the citizen hearings. This is the area that the school leader can least prepare for. Citizen hearings in most cases involve praise or concerns from the school community. The school leader welcomes praise and responds to concerns as well as he or she can. A citizen may complain about the service of the school district, or the union may cite some unfair practices. Unless the person at the helm of the meeting has some prior knowledge of these complaints and concerns, it will be a challenge to address them effectively.

Based on this brief description of the board meeting and its three major components, what should a school leader do to best prepare for the board meeting? Other variables being equal, prior information about the meeting is crucial. Sun Tzu wrote:

> You can obtain foreknowledge.
> You can't get it from demons or spirits.
> You can't see it from professional experience.
> You can't check it with analysis.
> You can only get it from other people.
> You must always know the enemy's situation.

(Gagliardi 2003, ch. 13)

The essence of Sun Tzu's wisdom here is to get foreknowledge, which means timely information. Timely information helps a leader make accurate decisions. In the Old Testament, when Moses explored the land of Canaan, he sent twelve men (spies) to find out about the people, the land, the soil, and the city. Specifically, Moses told the men to find out if the Canaanites were strong or weak, few or many; if the city was unfortified or fortified, the soil fertile or poor. Interestingly, Moses also asked the men to bring back some of the fruit of the land. Later, the fruit proved that Canaan is the land that flows with milk and honey.

> Be a smart commander and a good general.
> You do this by using your best and brightest people for spying.
> This is how you achieve the greatest success.
> This is how you meet the necessities of war.
> The whole army's position and ability to move depends on these spies.

> (Gagliardi 2003, ch. 13)

Sun Tzu specified the use of certain people called spies, those who could serve as a conduit of information. We have to be careful in applying this wisdom to education, though, because in education the use of information should not be secretive.

> You need a creative leader and a worthy commander.
> You must move your troops to the right places to beat others.
> You must accomplish your attack and escape unharmed.
> This requires foreknowledge.

> (Gagliardi 2003, ch. 13)

Sun Tzu explained that as leader and a commander, one relies on other people for timely information. Depending on your leadership position in the school organization, these people can be your supervisors, coworkers, subordinates, or other stakeholders of the school community. To ensure good communication, be sure you have good networking relationships with these people. They will be of great assistance to you with timely information and prepare you for a good board meeting.

Meetings are a significant part of communication, and therefore a significant responsibility of many school leaders is meeting assessment to ensure productivity. It will not be practical to assess all meetings or get feedback on every individual meeting. However, you might want to evaluate every fourth or fifth meeting using a specific multiple-choice format or an open-ended format. A multiple-choice format may contain items addressing the coverage of the agenda, the scheduling of the meeting, clarity of purpose, the preparation of the presenter(s), the execution of action items or decisions, and overall effectiveness. An open-ended format can ask about what was good about the meeting and for suggestions for the next meeting. In both assessment formats, ask for anonymous responses to ensure full and honest participation.

PRESENTATION AS A FORM OF COMMUNICATION

Presentation is something that is said, shown, or explained to an audience. Many people think of presentation as more formal because this is something that they experience in large, important group meetings.

Many school leaders are faced with preparing and doing a rather formal staff presentation at the beginning of the school year. The message presented usually is a mix of kick-off celebration, introduction of new staff, information sharing, and new directives for the school year. There are six questions that the leader should consider in the preparation and execution of a presentation:

1. Who is the audience?
2. What is the main message?
3. What are the parts of the message?
4. How are the parts organized?
5. What is the medium of presentation?
6. Who delivers the presentation?

In the classroom, we know the importance of aligning teaching and learning styles. To maximize learning, the teacher needs to align the instructional method and content as much as possible with the learning needs of the students. Similarly, the effective presenter knows the needs of the audience in order to grab their attention and interest. The audience could include new and tenured teachers, administrators, support

staff, and other paraprofessionals. When all these people gather together in a school auditorium on the opening day of school, what should
you focus on when talking to them in a large group? What should you
focus on if you break them into small groups? How do you effectively
group them? By grade level, content area, service area, etc.? Make sure
you know who is in the audience.

Next is the main message. It is the centerpiece; all the other presentation parts are only supportive in function. What you expect the audience to get out of the presentation is the main message. Meeting participants tend to pay most attention to the introduction and the conclusion
of the presentation. For that reason, the main message should be introduced first and then summarized in the conclusion. This way, the presenter hits the message at least twice. One question that the presenter
should answer when selecting the message is, "What is important and
relevant to the organization?" Using this criterion, the presenter emphasizes the importance and relevance of the message in both the introduction and conclusion. For example, many school presentations emphasize
the importance of student achievement, school improvement, and success. An introduction could be: "We had a very successful year of student
achievement, and this will help us to pass a school tax referendum for
building a new school." Or "This is our fourth year of not meeting the
adequate yearly progress. How can the school improve to avoid reorganization by the state?" How about an introduction about the improvement of the quality of school life, or the opportunity for advancement?
All in all, think seriously about the interests and concerns of the audience and be sure your message addresses them from the very start of the
presentation. When you capture the attention of the audience, you open
the floodgates to a successful presentation.

The message can be weak if it is not supported by explanations, examples, evidence, stories, analogies, and connections. The main message
is a general statement. The supports are specific statements. An effective
presenter makes these statements tactfully, as we will see in the following example. A good way to lead into the supports is to express briefly
and succinctly the point that you are going to make. This is a general
statement. It gives the audience a clear idea of where the speaker is in
the presentation. One should not underestimate the power of using sta-
tistical data. Data presentation is a specific statement. Data are objective

and give the audience facts rather than just another opinion. Student enrollment, demographics, test scores, and school budgets are examples of school data that one should use to support the message. The restatement of points is helpful. This will help the audience to transition from specifics back to the general statement. Where and how one strategically places the supportive components in the presentation helps the audience to understand, sustain, and amplify the message.

What is the medium of presentation? Audio, visual, and audience participation are some options. One suggestion is to use multisensory media and activities to engage the audience mentally and physically. PowerPoint presentations are a standard that audiences expect in large and small group meetings. Some audiences might even resent the presentation being anything less than a PowerPoint exhibit.

Have you seen a two-screen presentation at a conference? This is a communication method of overlapping the main topic with the topic of discussion. One method is to use one as the main directory and the other as the subdirectory. Figure 5.4 shows a two-screen presentation. The left screen is the main directory. This screen is up throughout the presentation to remind the audience about the main presentation outline. The right screen is the subdirectory. When someone arrives late at a presentation, he or she can look at the left screen to see the presentation outline and at the right screen to see the current discussion as it relates to the agenda. To do the two screens effectively, the presenter needs to be sure that the verbiage in the main and subdirectory is identical for clear transition (see arrow in figure 5.4). In Figure 5.4, the main directory screen on the left shows that the presentation topic is HELPING STUDENTS TO ACHIEVE. The screen on the right shows that the current discussion is "What do We Expect Students to Learn?" The two screens could be two flipcharts, or two overheads, or two photo slides. They work just the same. How can one get confused with the guidance of the two screens? For clear communication, your audience will know exactly where you are in the presentation even if the presentation is convoluted, they are not paying attention, or they are coming in late.

If you don't have an assistant to help you, learn how to prepare a PowerPoint presentation yourself.

Will the school leader be the presenter, or will he or she present with a team? The school leader approach lets people know who is in charge.

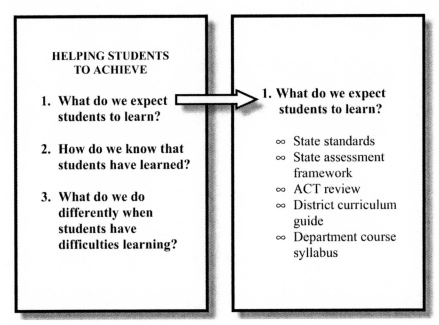

Figure 5.4.   A Two-Screen Presentation

A common example of a leader-led presentation is one done by the superintendent or the board of education. On the other hand, the team approach gives people the impression of collaboration. An example of a team approach is a presentation led by the school leader, followed by a teacher, such as the president of the union, and other staff representatives.

Read and analyze the PowerPoint presentation slides in figure 5.5. What is the main message? What are parts of the message, and how are they organized? How do the slides build the main message a little at a time? Where could one offer details and examples to support the message? How can this presentation be improved? Compare the presentation when it is delivered by a school leader versus by a school team. In either scenario, how can one make it equally effective?

There are a few rules to follow to create a powerful visual presentation. The first is to coordinate the visual (i.e., PowerPoint slide) with the presentation. Begin talking about the visual slide at the time that the slide is shown on the screen. Be sure that the audience is looking at what you are presenting. The second rule is to say what is written on the

Expectations & Accountability

Adult Basic Education
Triton College

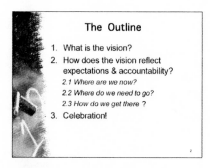

The Outline

1. What is the vision?
2. How does the vision reflect expectations & accountability?
   - 2.1 Where are we now?
   - 2.2 Where do we need to go?
   - 2.3 How do we get there ?
3. Celebration!

Triton COLLEGE

FIVE-YEAR VISION

Triton College is a Premier
Learner-Centered
Community College

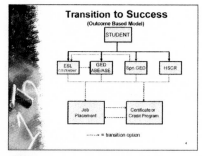

Transition to Success
(Outcome Based Model)

STUDENT

| ESL | GED ABE/ASE | Spn GED | HSCR |

Job Placement — Certificate or Credit Program

- - - → = transition option

Where Are We Now?

1. Enrollment = 6,074
2. ESL % of level completion >50%
3. GED completion % > 50%
4. P.D.= 25% attended in -service 3 times

*PROGRAM QUALITY GENERATES $

Where Do We Need to Go?

Achieve a higher level in

- student enrollment
- student retention
- student transition
- student support
- student goals
- student learning gains (ESL, GED)
- curriculum alignment
- professional development

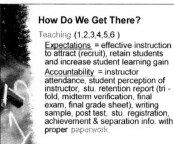

How Do We Get There?

Teaching (1,2,3,4,5,6)

Expectations = effective instruction to attract (recruit), retain students and increase student learning gain

Accountability = instructor attendance, student perception of instructor, stu. retention report (tri - fold, midterm verification, final exam, final grade sheet), writing sample, post test, stu. registration, achievement & separation info. with proper paperwork.

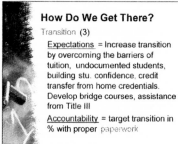

How Do We Get There?

Transition (3)

Expectations = Increase transition by overcoming the barriers of tuition, undocumented students, building stu. confidence, credit transfer from home credentials. Develop bridge courses, assistance from Title III

Accountability = target transition in % with proper paperwork

Figure 5.5. The Triton First Day of School PowerPoint Presentation

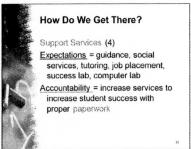

How Do We Get There?

Support Services (4)

Expectations = guidance, social
services, tutoring, job placement,
success lab, computer lab

Accountability = increase services to
increase student success with
proper paperwork

11

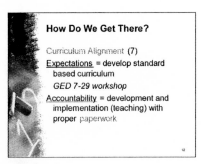

How Do We Get There?

Curriculum Alignment (7)

Expectations = develop standard
based curriculum

GED 7-29 workshop

Accountability = development and
implementation (teaching) with
proper paperwork

12

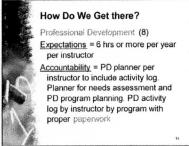

How Do We Get there?

Professional Development (8)

Expectations = 6 hrs or more per year
per instructor

Accountability = PD planner per
instructor to include activity log.
Planner for needs assessment and
PD program planning. PD activity
log by instructor by program with
proper paperwork

12

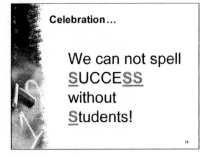

Celebration…

We can not spell
SUCCESS
without
Students!

12

Figure 5.5.   (*continued*)

visual. If the slide says, "expectations and accountability," say that as it appears on the screen, instead of saying, "what we want you to do and your responsibility to do it." The audience expects the presenter to say the exact words on the screen because many of them will read the words before the presenter speaks. Do not disappoint them. You could offer further explanations only after you say what is on the screen. The third rule is to scaffold the idea, building it a little at a time to expand it. Allow the audience a few seconds to read and understand the slide before the explanation. You might want to observe the five-second rule (i.e., count to 5) and allow five seconds of silence. Do not rush into discussing the slide while the audience is still trying to read the visual. Note that in figure 5.5 the first few slides speak to the concept of being student centered, and the last slide finishes with, "We cannot spell Success without students." In other words, you begin and finish with the same concept, thus reinforcing the message.

Regardless of the message, presenters are looking for a presentation formula that is easy to follow and understand. Little do they know that such a formula is connected closely to good teaching that is to the point and well organized. In the heart of a typical presentation is the main message, and the message is likely to have a number of ideas. How then do you get those ideas across, and how do you shift from one to the next?

One way to organize the presentation of ideas is the H.E.R.S. formula: Head's up of an idea, Evidence of the idea, Review of the idea, and Shift to the next idea. The audience is always interested to know ahead of time what you are planning to say in a presentation. To meet this anticipatory need, the presenter gives the audience a heads up to open each new section of the presentation. In short sentences, the presenter gives a succinct introduction of the idea. The heads up gives the audience a clear sense of where they are in the presentation. Some heads up phrases are, "The idea I am introducing is . . ." or "The first concept of my presentation is . . ." .

The mere introduction of an idea with no evidence to support it is weak. To push the idea forward, convincing evidence is needed, such as reports and examples. Examples of evidence are, "Here is a recent state school report card that shows . . ." and "Here is one school example that helps to support my idea about . . ." .

After being given several rounds of evidence and support, the audience may get distracted. For that reason there is a need to review what the original idea is about. At this point, restate the idea so people know you are transitioning from specific examples and stories back to the general idea statement. Examples are, "To restate the idea . . ." and "Allow me to summarize the idea at this time . . ." .

Give the audience a clear signal when you are ready to transition to a new idea. This signal tells the audience that you are moving from one idea to the next. Examples of transition phrases are, "Moving right along to the third idea . . ." and "This is a segue to the next idea . . ." .

The conclusion of a presentation is critical for leaving the audience with a good parting impression. An ideal conclusion reinforces and summarizes the main points of a presentation to ensure that the time spent was worthwhile. The conclusion of a presentation may include restating the challenge and rallying the audience to carry the ideas into actions. Impress the audience with the idea that mountains can be conquered. The use of personal words like *I* or *personally* in any conclusion statement are self-committing and risk taking, rather than egocentric. The words *we* and *our* are also appropriate after the use of *I* and *personally* to show the audience that you and the audience are a team. The exhibition of confidence by the presenter/leader here is what Sun Tzu described as wisdom and courage, among the winning factors discussed in chapter 1 of the *Art of War*. In summary, H.E.R.S. is one method to organize and guide your presentation so the audience can follow and understand easily.

Read and analyze the presentation below to see if you can find the important ingredients of a conclusion of a presentation by a new school administrator. Can you find the elements of challenge, future, optimism, future, commitment, and collaboration? How would you improve the conclusion and give it a better, more uplifting finish?

> For the new school semester, we are going to take on the challenge for a better future for our school. I am confident that I have your support because you know that I will fight for a higher level of achievement for our children and I am eager to do that with the support of all of you. I am honored to be the leader of this school as the school community sent a strong signal about the directions that they want me to lead the school. There is absolutely electrifying that we have a sense of new possibilities and of pride for what we can accomplish. I am honored to be a part of the school community and together we can achieve new heights of success. Thank you.

Most people dread being asked to make a presentation on the spot with absolutely no warning. On-the-spot presentations are difficult because there is little or no time for preparation. A general rule is not to refuse the request, which could indicate a lack of competence in your role as a school leader.

Okay, you are on, so what can you do? Let us assume that you were asked to give a report on a school initiative that you are in charge of and that you were not ready to give a full report about. You might review the four universal basic questions about any school initiative: (1) Where are we now? (2) Where do we want to go? (3) How do we get there? (4) How do we know that we are there? The confident presenter simply goes through the questions and gives a reasonable account for each. The fourth question may be the only one for which you do not have supporting data. Nevertheless, the impromptu presentation can be concluded by saying, "That's a quick view of the school initiative." A guiding principle for any impromptu presentation is to say something rather than nothing. To create a presentation from little preparation is another important ingredient of leadership, showing that you can think fast on your feet and stand and deliver—you're always prepared.

A good example of a presentation on the spot is the response that you give about school issues in a press conference. In a press conference the main body of information can be prepared ahead of time. The question-and-answer portion of the conference, however, is very similar to a presentation on the spot. The challenge is to say the right thing at the right time, or what is known as a politically correct response. School administrators should have no problem answering questions about school success and high student achievement. The comments should be connected back to the support of the school board of education and the efforts of the classroom teachers, as appropriate. On the other hand, a response to a scandal or some underachievement can be a problem. A guiding rule in a situation like is to respond on the positive side of the issue, using phrases like "less than satisfactory test results of the students . . ." rather than "the failure of students . . ." . Read and analyze the following press release about student achievement.

> The school did not make the achievement goals with our special needs students last year. We tested 98% of the 205 students in this group. Of these 40 percent of the students have severe cognitive disabilities and another 9% with learning disabilities. Our special education staff and regular education staff work with these students continuously to make sure students have steady learning progress. Nevertheless, it is a challenge for some students, especially those with severe cognitive disabilities to meet the predetermined achievement goals. A review of the student progress from the past three years shows that these students are learning and mastering skills that will enable them to function successfully in our school community.

The information in the press release is first and foremost factual. It is both honest and accurate. After the main message of student achievement not meeting the goals, the presentation covers the composition and characteristics of the students. It finishes on a confident and positive note that the improvement efforts are continuous and there is hope for future success. For questions that one is in no position to respond to, one has to resort to "It is not appropriate to comment at this time."

READING SIGNALS AS A FORM OF COMMUNICATION

When there is much running about and the soldiers fall into rank,
It means that the critical moment has come . . . .
When the soldiers stand leaning on their spears,
They are faint from want of food . . . .
The sight of men whispering together in small knots or speaking in subdued
    tones points to disaffection amongst the rank and file.

(Gagliardi 2003, ch. 9)

In chapter 9 of the *Art of War*, Sun Tzu discussed the reading or hearing of nonverbal communications in the battlefield. These nonverbal communications or signals include movements among the trees of a forest, showing the advancement of enemy; the rising of startled birds in their flight, showing the imminence of an ambush; and dust rising in a high column, showing the advance of chariots. More interestingly, Sun Tzu also discussed and interpreted the verbal and nonverbal behaviors of soldiers. In Sun Tzu's time, the accurate reading of signals meant adjusting battle strategies to win. Misreading of signals could be fatal, resulting in defeat and the loss of many lives.

Reading, hearing, and interpretation of signals in the forms of eye contact, tone of voice, gestures, and facial expression are important nonverbal communication skills in the real work world. One does not necessarily put all one's thoughts into words. Much of our thoughts are expressed nonverbally, letting people know we are friendly, confrontational, businesslike, courteous, agitated, dominant, passive, assertive, and much more. That being said, it is very important that the effective school leader know how to use proper signals and also be able to read signals from others.

Good eye contact is crucial for capturing the attention of an audience. For one thing, the audience pays close attention to the appearance of the presenter when he or she approaches the podium, closing in on the presenter's face and zeroing in on the presenter's eyes. Some common mistakes of poor eye contact include the presenter spending too much time looking at the visuals or reading the speech or gazing at the fixtures of the room, avoiding eye contact with people. A presenter with poor eye contact is perceived as having low self-esteem or lacking confidence.

Why is good eye contact important in a presentation? The answer is simply to get clues from the audience to see if, for example, they need more information, because they are asking their neighbors for clarification; or if the presenter needs to speed up a little because people are getting bored; or if the audience needs a break, because people are leaving to use the facilities. During a presentation, make an attempt to look everyone in the eyes. Do not overlook the people in the back or in the far corners of the room. By maintaining good eye contact, you are communicating with them nonverbally.

A skilled keynoter with an extensive linguistic background said "good morning" in twenty-five different intonations at a professional conference. The inflections of his voice fully communicated the message in various ways, from cheerful to angry and many other moods in between. As a rule, a wide range of voice intonation is preferred over a monotone. A notable difference between a good presenter and a boring presenter is the range of voice inflection. Watch television newscasters and listen to how they fluctuate their voices to make the news fresh and exciting. Better still, watch thirty-second television commercials and learn how the announcer uses his or her voice to sell the product or the service with real conviction and enthusiasm.

WRITING AS A FORM OF COMMUNICATION

Writing is printed words, letters, sentences, and paragraphs conveying thoughts, ideas, experiences, insights, and learning. The school leader uses a variety of forms of writing to communicate to people in the organization. The school leader writes a business document, a presentation, a grant application, a newsletter, an interoffice memo, a letter, and many other documents to different audiences for different purposes. Many people think of writing as similar to speaking, but that is not quite correct. Unlike conversation, writing is more formal. For that reason, writing as one speaks might not be acceptable in the business world. To generate thoughts, the writer brainstorms a map of ideas from an anchor topic. The anchor topic represents the message.

A school principal needs to write a memo to the school staff to prepare and organize them for a professional development meeting in four weeks. The topic of the training is effective instruction. To brainstorm on the topic, the school principal thinks of a large group, all-staff presentation and several breakout sessions for the grade levels. For each individual session, who, when, where, how, and what come to mind. An idea map is developed based on these thoughts. An examination of figure 5.6 shows that the map is a graphic representation of ideas in cluster. The map allows one to express with both language and design. One characteristic of an idea map is an informal and fun expression that is not restricted by organization and writing mechanics. For example, the design of the map may start from a topic in the center of the page. Ideas related to the topic may radiate from the center like the spokes of a wheel. Or the topic might start from one side of a page and move to the other side of the page with clusters of connecting ideas. The design

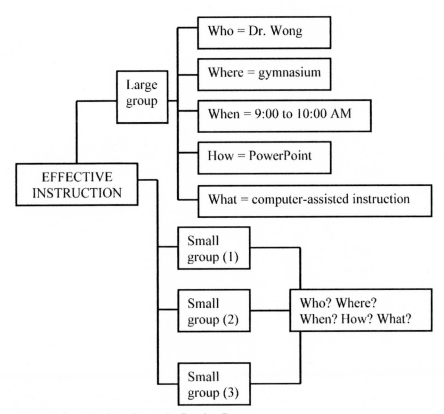

Figure 5.6.   Idea Map for an In-Service Day

options are limited only by one's imagination. After the composition of the idea map, it is a matter of simply transferring from the map into words—writing.

Another way to start the writing process is to ask questions, which when answered can become the framework of the writing. An author was interested in writing a children's book about the giant pandas. In the brainstorming process, he asked himself eight questions about the giant panda:

1. What is the giant panda?
2. What is the history of the giant panda?
3. Where do giant pandas live?
4. What are the eating habits of the giant pandas?
5. How do giant pandas communicate?
6. How do giant pandas defend themselves?
7. How intelligent are giant pandas?
8. Is the giant panda an endangered species?

Extensive research was done to find answers to these questions. When the answers were organized, each question became a chapter of the book. Finally a book with eight chapters, entitled *Giant Panda*, was published (Wong 1987).

Ask yourself questions before you write. When you ask questions, you are in fact brainstorming before writing. Planning by brainstorming before you write will make the actual writing less challenging. Use the writing brainstorming sheet (table 5.3). You will find the sheet an easy guide for your writing assignment.

The organization of the brainstorming sheet is unique in that it asks questions about both the reader and the writer (i.e., the writing). The writer needs to know who the reading audience is; as Sun Tzu suggested, know your enemy, although the reader is not here perceived as the enemy. Many successful writers write for an audience, and there is a correlation between how much the writer knows about the audience and how successful he or she is. The more the writer knows about the "relative positions" of the reader, the more successful he or she will become. Is the audience a superior, colleague, or subordinate? Obviously the format of the writing will be adjusted to the formality of the audi-

Table 5.3. Writing Brainstorming Sheet

WRITING BRAINSTORMING SHEET	
(1) About the Reader	
1.1 Who is/are the reader(s)?	
1.2 Readers' previous knowledge of the topic?	
1.3 Readers' opinions/concerns about the topic?	
(2) About the Writing	
2.1 What is the writing topic?	
2.2 What is the writing goal?	
2.3 Resources?	
2.4 What is the writing format?	
2.5 What is the message?	
2.6 What are the supports of the message?	

ence. Adjusting the format and content to the audience is a good application of "know yourself and know the enemy." Is your overall goal of writing to inform or to persuade? How much information is enough and how much is not enough depends on your alignment and understanding of the prior knowledge of the audience. If the purpose of the writing is to persuade, be sure that there are adequate supports. If the purpose of the writing is to inform, be sure that you also explain the information at the right level because adult readers do not like to be treated as if they are children. In an information memorandum to the office staff, a supervisor tells the staff about a personnel reorganization of the office and explains the reasons behind the decision. The reasons explained are related to resource limitations and promotion of student achievement, addressing possible staff questions at the intellectual, emotional, and personal levels.

Many people recognize grant writing as the ultimate writing challenge because good and clear writing is rewarded with funds. Grant writing is an excellent example of communication to reach a level of mutual understanding. In these days of limited resources, seeking external funds is common for school organizations, especially large ones. Grant writing is often done by professionals with such titles as director of development and director of planning. However, more and more grant writing is being done by administrative staff members who wear one or two other hats. Regardless of who the grant writer is, that person has to be a good communicator not only in writing but also with other people. The first quality of good writing is that it is easy to understand. Proposal writing should not be done in an office, remote from the rest of the organization. The second quality of being a good people communicator is becoming apparent and critical. Let us look into the four principles and six components of grant writing.

The four basic principles of grant writing are similar to those of any good persuasive writing:

- **Write to the point.** Clear communication is what writing to the point is about. Sometimes it is difficult to determine the quality of the proposal by its length. A two-page proposal may bore the reader, while a twenty-page proposal may entice the reader to look for more. Many grant organization limits the length of the proposal to a predetermined number of pages. Express your thoughts clearly, and stay within the limits. You would not like to invalidate your proposal by not following the grant writing specifications.
- **Stay positive.** Be upbeat in the grant writing experience and remember that this is not like writing home for money. In other words, you do not have to beg, and you do not have to apologize. Instead, you are an aspiring applicant offering the funding agency the opportunity to be a partner in important and purposeful activities. Funding organizations are more than willing to fund winners, not losers. Stay positive.

- **Support your assumptions.** Unsupported assumptions commonly find their way into grant proposals. These assumptions can be lack of support for a causal relationship or lack of information about the school organization. Do not assume the funding agencies know anything about your organization; often they do not. Have you seen grant applications in which the writer leads into an assumption by saying "the organization believes"? Lack of support for an assumption is a check on writing logic and coherence by the grant reader.
- **Write in comprehensible English.** The point here is to write without using jargon. If you must use things like acronyms, define them in simple terms. To test the clarity of your writing, have a colleague read the proposal and ask him or her to comment on what is not clear. Better still, ask a colleague from outside your department who is unfamiliar with the proposal to read it. This way, the person helping will not have any preconceptions or operating assumptions about the proposal.

There are eight components of grant writing (see figure 5.7): summary, introduction, needs assessment, goals and objectives, methods, promise to sustain, evaluation, and budget. The components are sequential and are organized to obtain the support of the funding agency.

Summary

Grant writing is unique because the summary appears at the beginning and it is often referred to as the executive summary. A summary at the beginning of the proposal is important because it is often required by the funding agency; it is the first piece and may be the only thing that

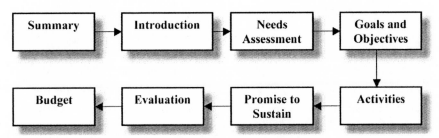

Figure 5.7.   The Eight Components of a Grant Proposal

the reviewer will read; and it is the advanced organizer that puts what follows into a frame. Let us read, analyze, and compare two examples and determine the characteristics of a good summary.

Example A.   The goal of this proposal is to assist special needs students in School District 8 to improve their skills in learning. These learning skills include team collaboration, acute decision making, and thinking independently and creatively. It is hoped that the program will help students to become lifelong learners and participate in democratic citizenship, with the support funding of $60,000.

Example B.   School District 8 in Panada Village currently runs a supplemental EXCEL program for 612 students between the ages of 8 and 10. Forty-three percent of the 612 students were diagnosed last year with learning disabilities. The students are in dire need of appropriate learning accommodation. Appropriate learning accommodation offered by the classroom teachers can increase the level of operation to allow them to develop their potential and attend regular education classes. The State Department of Education has recognized that accommodation services are effective in the early, formative years of students. This proposal would expand the special needs services of School District 8. The total cost of the program is $100,000. Of this, $40,000 has already been committed by the Panada School Board of Education. This proposal is requesting the balance needed, $60,000.

In essence, a good summary should include the identification of the applicant, the reason for the grant request, the goals to be accomplished, activities to support the goals, and the cost of the project. Putting yourself in the shoes of a grant reader, would you consider funding Example A or Example B? Explain the reasons for your choice.

Introduction

The introduction requirements of a grant proposal vary depending on whether the proposal is sent to a government agency or a private organization. For a government agency, you might be asked to provide background information on the applicant. For a private foundation, the introduction is usually extensive because the applicant needs to establish its qualifications and credibility.

The introduction starts your grant proposal and is a critical section to encourage the reader to read on or set it aside. Start with something upbeat, like a quote from a recent newspaper article describing the many good things your school has accomplished. Other things that you can put in the introduction are accomplishments and impact, significant events, positive comments from other organizations, results from accreditation evaluations of your programs, and important publications from your schools. When you strategize what to include in the introduction, keep two things in mind. First, there needs to be a balance of quotes and statistics. Second, focus on your credibility in the area in which you are asking the funding agency to support you. Convince the grant reader that you are willing and able to carry out the tasks in the proposal successfully. Another way to enhance the credibility of the organization is to attach endorsement letters. A good letter of endorsement will even commit to some level of support should the proposal be funded. You could check your introduction to see if it is interesting, free of jargon, and brief and to the point, and most of all whether it provides a logical transition to the next section, the problem statement or needs assessment.

Needs Assessment

The needs assessment of the proposal explains why the grant writer is being asked to provide funds support. If you were a philanthropist, wouldn't you want to know why an organization was asking you for money? The needs assessment describes the conditions of a place (i.e., schools) and certain people (i.e., students), at a specific time (i.e., the previous three years), with a certain need (i.e., students falling behind in their mathematics skills). In other words, the needs assessment describes the situation that caused the grant writer to write the grant proposal. The term *needs assessment* is used interchangeably with *problem statement*. Some important elements of a needs assessment that grant readers pay attention to are statements relating to the goal of the organization, supporting documentation or statistics, input from clients, and the plausibility of implementing the program if it is funded. When you are done writing a needs statement, ask yourself the following questions: "What is the need (or problem) that the organization is focusing on? Who will benefit from the funding? What directions are the needs leading in?"

Goals and Objectives

Goals are long-range aims and purposes. Effective program goals are S.M.A.R.T:

SPECIFIC: Goals are clear, with end results.

MEASURABLE: Goals are achieved because one can see or count the results.

ATTAINABLE: Goals are doable with available resources.

RELEVANT: Goals align with the direction of the organization.

TIME-BOUND: Goals are achieved in a defined time frame.

As some people say, "If you do not know where you are going, any road will take you there." Goals that are not S.M.A.R.T. are similar to taking any road to reach a destination. Program goals that are measurable are cut down into short-term objectives; this should be one criterion that you use to determine whether a program is effective. Measurable objectives answer the questions, "Where do we plan to go, and how do we know when we get there?" Let us look at an example.

At the completion of a one-week professional development workshop, a minimum of 25 percent of the teacher participants will demonstrate a 40 percent gain on the Aim High Grant Writing Test, including skills in writing the (a) summary, (b) introduction, (c) needs assessment, (d) goals, (e) activities, (f) evaluation, and (g) budget.

Goals and objectives are weak if they are not supported by activities. People often confuse activities with goals and objectives. The difference between a goal or an objective and activities is the difference between means and ends. What is your assessment of the following objective statement?

The objective of the proposal is to increase the opportunity of special needs students to participate in the EXCEL program by employing a team of special education staff who will conduct training sessions for the district's teachers.

How do you measure the "increased opportunity"? The objective of increasing the opportunity is not really measurable. The objective statement is not well defined according to the measurable criterion. Let us look at another objective statement.

The proposed program in SD 88 has the primary objective to increase the percentage of special education to regular education transition from the current 5 percent per year to 20 percent in three years.

Does the objective statement better answer the questions, "Where do we plan to go, and how do we know when we get there?"

Are the set goals and objectives attainable? Grave mistakes are made when the goal is too ambitious to attain. Sun Tzu wrote:

You go hundreds of miles to fight for an advantage.
Then the enemy catches your commanders and your army.
Your strong soldiers get there first.
Your weaker soldiers follow behind.
Using this approach, only one in ten will arrive.
You can try to go fifty miles to fight for an advantage.
Then your commander and army will stumble.
Using this method, only half of your soldiers will make it.
You can try to go thirty miles to fight for an advantage.
Then only two out of three get there.
If you make your army travel without good supply lines, your army will die.
Without supplies and food, your army will die.
If you don't save the harvest, your army will die.

(Gagliardi 2003, ch. 7)

In chapter 7, Sun Tzu warned against setting high and unreachable goals. On ancient battlefields, a hundred miles was a lot for horses and foot soldiers. The consequence of marching long distances was that the enemy could capture the exhausted troops, and the chance of victory was only 10 percent. However, when the army marched less distance, such as fifty miles, the chance of victory chance increased to 50 percent. Finally, when the army marched only thirty miles, the troops remained strong and fresh, and the victory rate would increase to 75 percent! Resources were considered next. An army will die if its supply lines are severed. Similarly, a goal with no resource support is not attainable. In grant writing, the writer is requesting funding for more resource support. Such resource support can be personnel, technology, training, and/or release time.

In summary, when writing a program objective, check to see that it is specific, measurable, attainable, relevant, and time bound.

Activities

Activities should develop directly from the goals and objectives. Ordinarily, this is a presentation of what will happen in the program. Let us look at the following example.

SD 88 Title I program is designed to improve the mathematics achievement of elementary level special needs students in six elementary schools. This proposal has a focus on staff development to apply the concept of using mathematics specialists to assist classroom staff in diagnosing student strengths and weaknesses, as well as the development of supporting instructional materials.

SD 88 Title I program will employ a cadre of 12 mathematics specialists. These mathematics specialists are certified teachers with a minimum of 18 college credit hours in mathematics content and teaching methods. They also have the additional qualification of staff training with the integrated use of instructional technology. Teaching staff receiving the training will have a work experience of at least five years in SD 88, with tenure status in the department of compensatory education.

To maximize the success of the mathematics training program, SD 88 will train the lead teachers in the primary grades using the "train the trainer" model. These trained lead teachers will then train the grade-level teachers in the small learning communities at their respective schools. The training will include the assessment of mathematics skills of students, with the development of appropriate differentiated instructional methods and supplementary materials. The training will occur throughout the coming school year, September through May. An activity calendar is in Appendix A of this proposal.

A small learning community has the advantage over more-traditional training programs because it addresses the individual needs of teachers in a small group setting with reference to grade level expertise. SD 88's efforts to date have demonstrated the potential of this program to increase student success. Of 500 students who participated in a pilot program last year, 300, or 60 percent, successfully transitioned to general education classes and passed the annual state mandatory examination.

What one gathers from the activities section of the program description are the key components of staff selection, staff training, and participant selection, and selection of the training model (i.e., small learning communities).

In essence, check the activity section of the program to see that the program activities are succinctly described and include the sequence of activities, the selection and training of staff, and the reasons for the selection. The S.M.A.R.T. ingredients can also be used to guide the description of the program activities.

Promise to Sustain

Grant funding agencies often ask whether the funding recipient or organization can sustain and continue the efforts after the grant money runs out. It would be a disaster to bring a successful program to a screeching halt for lack of continuous funding. The funding organization is concerned about supporting an organization if its efforts cannot be continued. Here, the funding agencies are paying attention to long-term impact rather than short-term success. No funding agency would like to adopt any organization as a long-term dependent. What can a grant writer say about the promise of future funding? Where will the grant writer find funding beyond the current grant?

A grant writer can seek future funding support in a number of ways. If your funded program is successful, and if you are a large enough school organization, the school organization itself might be able to assume the responsibilities of future funding. The best way to present this proposal is to show that you have a track record of doing that successfully in the past. It is simply not convincing if you write, "We will attempt to look for future sources of support." Does your school organization have a fund-raising program, such as an institutional foundation or Parent Teacher Organization? Can you demonstrate the ability of your foundation program to raise money for future program support? If so, this is a definite way to secure future funding. Do you have another funding source? Can they help to support you with future funding?

These are all possibilities, and the more specific you can be, the more confidence you will instill in the grant reader. The plan for future support provides the guarantee of future funding, community interest, and the continuation of the program. Read the following example.

> School District 88 is requesting seed money to improve the mathematics achievement of 100 special needs students, and the program will require more funding if its effectiveness is demonstrated. Two sources that future funding support are being sought:
>
> (I) From the local Parent Teacher Organization (PTO)
>   The SD 88 PTO has agreed to set aside 35 percent of its annual revenue to support the improvement of mathematics achievement of special needs students. The PTO has also agreed to volunteer its personnel to assist with the program logistics during the five-day summer staff professional development workshop.
> (II) From current funding agencies
>   The State Board of Education is a current funding agency for the mathematics improvement of our general education students, and they have committed to supporting the training project by providing two cost-free university mathematics education consultants in collaboration with the state university system. The amount of this contribution is approximately $5,000.

Evaluation

Evaluation determines the level of program success in terms of the process and the products. Questions asked in the process evaluation include, "Is the program conducted in a manner consistent with the plan?" and "What is the correlation between program activities and program success?" Questions asked in product evaluation include, "How successful is the program in attaining its stated goals and objectives?" and "How successful are the goals and objectives attributed to the program?"

There are many reasons to include evaluation in the grant proposal, other than the obvious one that it is required by the funding organization. These include quality control by the applicant, examination of the stated objectives and their accountability, determination of costs and benefits, sincerity and diligence of the applicant, and determination of program reliability. Evaluation is an accountability component of the

Table 5.4.   Objective Data Measure

Objective	Data	Data Procedure	Measure
Increase student success in math by 20 percent in one semester	Reported math pre- and post-test scores	Collect pre-test score in fall and post-test score in spring from teachers' record book	Compare the pre- and post-test scores

grant proposal. If the goal of the proposed program is to train teachers in new mathematical skills, then the obvious evaluation question would be, "How many teachers, or what percentage of the teachers, will be trained?" or "How will the training impact the mathematics achievement of students?" In table 5.4, look at the flow of the stated objective in relationship to what data to collect, how they are collected, and how they are measured.

In developing the evaluation, a grant writer must consider the alignment of the measure to the goals and objectives. For example, if the goals and objectives are stated in the improvement of a process, then the evaluation will be an evaluation of the process. Do not use a product measure to evaluate a process, and vice versa. It is possible to administer both a process evaluation and a product evaluation, depending on what is stated in the goals and the objectives. Be sure you are clear and accurate about what you need to measure.

Either an internal or an external evaluator may be used. There are pros and cons for both, related to the degree of subjectivity or objectivity desired as well as to cost-effectiveness. Consider how you need to collect the data for evaluation with reference to the resources and the nature of the program. Different analysis techniques require different methods of data collection. Some common methods of collecting evaluation data are pre-post test comparison, evaluator observation, interviews, and client opinion survey (Wong and Lam 2007).

Budget

If you request a sum of $189,150 to support the operation of a program, what will that entail? Answering this question requires some degree of specificity because you have to tell the grant reader how the money will be broken down into different categories, such as personnel, non-personnel, and indirect costs. The degree of budget specificity reflects the quality of planning and might encourage confidence in the grant reader. An example of nonspecific or even sloppy budgeting is a budget for miscellaneous items or contingency funds. Budgets should be built from the ground up. In other words, a budget is based on the set goals, the objectives, and the methodology that the grant writer proposed. In that context, the grant writer should review, summarize, and itemize such things as staffing, facilities, equipment, supplies, professional development, and so on. It is important that the grant writer complete this list in the development of a budget. Otherwise unrealistic requests, in which budget and program are not related, could jeopardize the chance of funding. Some funding agencies require a specific format for the budget proposal. If a format is required, that format is what you will follow. Let us take a look at the development of a budget to illustrate the three basic components of personnel, non-personnel, and indirect costs (figure 5.8).

In the personnel section of the budget should be listed all full- and part-time staff in the proposed program. The information should include the title or position of staff, the number of persons per title, the salary (monthly or yearly as appropriate), and the total amount. If any staff member is to be paid out of a local funding source, that information should be put in a separate column, labeled local share or in-kind

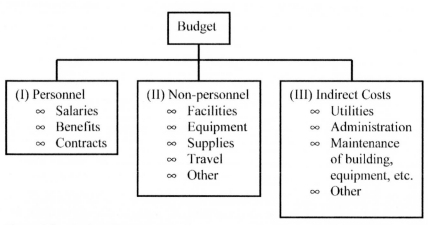

Figure 5.8.   Budget Components

contribution. To determine the salary of a staff member, you might want to compare the position to a similar one in a similar agency, to get a realistic figure. If you proposed using volunteers in your program, you will be asked to deliver the promised volunteer services, just as if the funding source were actually paying salaries. Document the volunteer hours and be able to provide that evidence in the case of an audit.

Employee fringe benefits vary from state to state, and some are mandatory. Mandatory benefits may include insurance or state unemployment coverage. Such benefits are normally based on a percentage of salary (e.g., 10 percent), although some are a flat amount per month per staff person. As with salary, the benefits should be comparable to the benefits offered in similar organizations in the community. The following personnel budget example shows that there are one full-time director and one office assistant, three instructors, and one instructional aide, at a total personnel cost of $135,300.

(a) Salaries	
1 director @$2,500/month × 12 months	$ 30,000
1 office assistant @$1,500/month × 12 months	$ 18,000
3 instructors @$2,000/month × 12 months	$ 72,000
1 instructional aide @200 hours per year × $15/hour	$ 3,000
Subtotal	$123,000
(b) Benefits	
10% of $123,000	$ 12,300
Total Personnel Cost	$135,300

The rent paid for the facilities or the valuation of the donated facilities may be listed in the non-personnel section. Again, the estimated cost should be comparable to prevailing costs in the area in which you are located. In the operation of a grant-funded program, the equipment may be either leased or purchased. This cost may also be listed under non-personnel. Use your discretion in this part of the budget. Make a sincere effort obtain as much donated equipment as you can to lower the funding costs, as well as to show that other contributing partners are helping to make the program work. Read the grant guidelines carefully for the definition of equipment. "Equipment" is usually defined as something that costs more than $500 per piece or has a life span of more than a year. Supplies are non-personnel items, such as desktop or office supplies. This category may also include publications, journal subscriptions, and postage. Transportation costs in general are included in the non-personnel category. This could include staff or consultant travel costs. Be sure that you use the per diem (hotel and meals) rate appropriate for the location. There is yet another catch-all category, which includes tuition for classes, professional association dues, and printing. List the costs in as much detail as you know rather than lumping them together in a miscellaneous and ill-defined category.

The third budget component is indirect costs, which may be defined as costs that are not readily identifiable with a specific program or activity but are necessary to the normal operation of the organization. It may not be possible to charge a cost directly to a line item. The expense to operate and maintain buildings and equipment is an example of indirect cost. How about the depreciation of building and equipment? This is also an indirect cost. Indirect cost is an area that is not generally well understood, but it should be explored to fully benefit the proposed program.

The personnel, non-personnel, and indirect cost components are brought together in the sample budget below. The line items of the budget are quite specific. Each line item details the unit cost (e.g., $2,500 per month for one staff person), a specified period of time (e.g., twelve months), and the cost of the item. Adding all the line items together gives us the total amount of the budget.

MAKING DECISIONS AS A FORM OF COMMUNICATION

Effective leaders make sound and timely decisions and communicate them clearly to stakeholders. Behind the sound and timely decisions are the courage and authority of the leader. Will the courageous leader use the authority he or she has been given to make decisions, or hesitate for fear of making a mistake? As a general rule, the higher the position, the more power the leader will have to make bigger and more important decisions without undue outside interference. In other words, the higher position gives the person the power that he or she needs to get things

SAMPLE BUDGET

(I) *Personnel*

(a) Salaries

1 director @$2,500/month × 12 months	$ 30,000
1 office assistant @$1,500/month × 12 months	$ 18,000
3 instructors @$2,000/month × 12 months	$ 72,000
1 instructional aide @200 hours per year × $15/hour	$ 3,000

(b) Benefits

10% of $123,000	$ 12,300

(c) Purchased Services

1 consultant @$500/day × 10 days	$ 5,000
1 project auditor @$2,000	$ 2,000

(II) *Non-personnel*

(a) Office

Rent $2,000/month × 12 months	$ 24,000
Utilities @$500/month × 12 months	$ 6,000
Telephone@200/month × 12 months	$ 2,400

(b) Equipment

Word processor/printer	$ 5,000
Furniture (5 desk/chair sets @ $750)	$ 3,750

(c) Supplies

Desktop supplies @$200/year/staff × 12 months	$ 1,200

(d) Travel

3 Chicago-San Diego roundtrip airfares @500/each	$ 1,500
10 days per diem (San Diego) @$200/day	$ 2,000

(III) *Indirect costs*

Office insurance	$ 700
Conference registration @$100 each for 3 instructors	$ 300
TOTAL PROJECT COST	$189,150

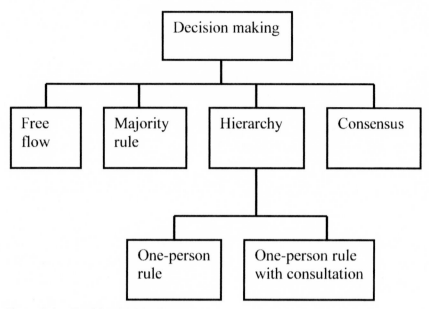

Figure 5.9. Decision-Making Types

done. Leaders use various methods of decision making (see figure 5.9). Look at figure 5.9 to see which method reflects your decision-making style and which is most effective as a form of communication.

The first type of decision making has no structure; it is free flow in nature. The decision-making group members trust each other to make a decision for the common good. The free-flow climate also fosters few rules and penalties. In this process, decisions are often made by a few dominant or assertive stakeholders. Many quick and informal decisions are made this way by leaders who are less conforming and unrestricted in spirit.

The second type is majority rule decision making. Many people are familiar with this type of decision making from public school board meetings. In a typical meeting, the members follow the parliamentary procedure to work with each other in a reasonably orderly fashion. Nevertheless, this type of decision making divides the group into winners and losers, with inherent competition and struggles for power because the final decision may include the ineffective ingredients of the winning proposal and exclude the effective ingredients of the losing proposal. The effective school leader usually discusses an issue or a problem in prior board subcommittee meetings before bringing them to the public meeting for a final vote. In this way the leader prepares the board members and gives them a heads up to avoid prolonged and unnecessary debate at the public meeting. The majority rule model works with any size group, and the decision is made final by voting.

The third method is hierarchy decision making. The hierarchy follows an explicit chain of command, which can be autocratic or consultative. An autocrat is one person who rules, with that person usually located at the top of the command chain, such as the president of the board or the superintendent of schools. Many decisions are made daily to sustain the effective operation of a school. If the school administrator has to run the decisions through committees, the school will suffer, because there are only so many work hours in a day. So the school administrator makes autocratic decisions, and that is quite acceptable. The consultative hierarchy also involves one person ruling, but with the assistance of experts.

The Eagle Ridge School District for many years was plagued by the ineffectiveness of central office personnel. The superintendent hired a director to replace a retiree and at the same time seek advice from external consultants to reorganize the central office. The reorganization decisions subsequently made were perceived as having been made in consultation with experts; however, it could well have been a directive from the superintendent, who simply disguised the decision as an expert consultation. Sun Tzu interpreted this maneuvering strategy as "killing someone with a borrowed dagger."

The fourth method is consensus decision making. This process is a mutual search for solutions until the best one for the group emerges—a decision that all can accept. This process is very time consuming and sometimes frustrating because conflicts are brought into the open and minority ideas are considered, with strong encouragement for cooperation.

Which decision method fits the Chinese proverb, "A single arrow is easily broken, but not ten in a bundle?" Which is the right one for you? To make that choice you will need to answer the ultimate question: "Whose responsibility is it to make the decision?" In other words, must the leader make this decision, or could someone else do it? To answer this question accurately, the leader must clearly understand his or her job description and know which decisions he or she alone must make and which staff members may make.

A Hamilton middle school principal reflected on a tough decision he had to make about releasing a teacher from his duty. The situation came up when a group of parents visited the principal to complain about the lack of order and the subsequent lack of learning in a particular class. The principal listened to make sure he understood all the facts and the legitimacy of the concern. He visited the class several times to verify the complaints and finally invited the teacher to his office for a meeting. It was a fact that the teacher was not effective and was the cause of the problem. Should the principal protect the interest of the teacher, or should he protect the interest of the students? The principal upheld his charge and responsibilities and decided that the teacher should go, yet he gave the teacher a chance at remediation. He suggested a number of options and directed the teacher to follow through. The principal made it clear that if the teacher failed to meet the remediation requirements, then his job would be terminated. The process was documented and signed by both the principal and the teacher.

There is an unfortunate and a fortunate ending to this story. The unfortunate part is that the teacher was not successful in the remediation process and was recommended to be fired. The fortunate part is that the teacher in question was actually eligible for early retirement. In the final analysis, the principal made a win-win decision to convince the teacher to take early retirement and then replaced him. The decision allowed the teacher to save face and renewed the impetus of effective learning in the classroom. In the Hamilton school situation, the decision was made by the school principal alone.

In another case, an assistant superintendent of teaching and learning was given the charge to make a recommendation to the school board to adopt a new mathematics text series that would augment student mathematics achievement. The assistant superintendent reviewed the state mathematics learning standards to understand the specific state requirements. Through the learning standards review, he succinctly defined the mathematics knowledge and skills areas of proficiency that students must meet and exceed. In addition to the standards review, the assistant superintendent read widely in education and math research journals to broaden his understanding of the mathematics texts used in the state and across the nation, to see how others dealt with similar situations in the adoption of a new mathematics series to align teaching with learning standards. The assistant superintendent then assembled facts bearing on the final decision to adopt. He collected second- or even third-hand information by reading and studying. Next, he asked questions of people who were using the top five math series as recommended by the professional research, and he narrowed his choice to three. From there, the assistant superintendent called a teacher committee to pilot the three texts to further collect data on their impact on student achievement, ease of use, and the implications for professional development and the use of resources.

The assistant superintendent let the teachers know that they were a meaningful part of the decision and that he would not lead too far ahead of the troops, where he might be perceived as the enemy. At the conclusion of a four-month pilot, the teacher committee shared and synthesized its findings. The final adoption decision was thoroughly thought out, and the commitment to carry out the decision was promoted. This decision was made by the assistant superintendent in collaboration with the teaching staff. Which type of decision was it?

As can be seen from these real-world examples, decision making can be very difficult, mainly because of the fear of making mistakes. However, hesitating to decide is also a decision. Effective school leaders do not waver; they move forward with confidence and take sound and timely action to accomplish what is best for the students and the organization. They collect all the appropriate information possible and then, as Sun Tzu would have advised, have the courage and the authority to say, "Now it is up to me to decide what to do."

REFLECTIONS ON A GOOD COMMUNICATOR

Different forms of communication, such as chain of command, meeting, presentation, writing, and decision making, have been discussed in this chapter to show their complexity and challenges. Until communication is used and practiced, the skills will not be learned and mastered. Mistakes are the best teachers. Leadership is about developing good working relationships, and the heart of relationships is effective communication.

It is only appropriate to examine your current communication practices at the end of this chapter. The purpose of this assessment is to determine where you are now to establish a baseline for continuous improvement. Answer the following true or false questions.

---

1. Listening is important when you anticipate what your colleague is going to say.

   True ___   False ___

2. A key message is easier to understand and remember if you reinforce and repeat it.

   True ___   False ___

3. Asking a person to summarize what you said is a good way to check whether that person understands the message.

   True ___   False ___

4. It is okay to interrupt a long-winded person in a conversation to paraphrase what he or she has said.

   True ___   False ___

5. Technical information, such as the operation of a new computer program, is more likely to be understood if you tell people to listen attentively.

   True ___   False ___

6. You build a good relationship with another person working in the organization through communication.

   True ___   False ___

7. The principles of large group communication and of small group communication are very different.

   True ___   False ___

8. A clear chain of command enhances the chance of effective communication.

   True ___   False ___

9. Being reactive is more effective than being proactive in communication.

   True ___   False ___

---

10. Calling a meeting for the sake of having a meeting is a good guideline.

    True ___ False ___

11. At the end of a presentation it is good to let the audience know how they can benefit from the information.

    True ___ False ___

12. Grant writing is narrative writing.

    True ___ False ___

13. You cannot quantify the results of a S.M.A.R.T. goal, although the goal is attainable.

    True ___ False ___

14. In the case of a bomb threat, the best way to make a decision is to establish an emergency committee.

    True ___ False ___

REFERENCES

Gagliardi, Gary. 2003. *The* Art of War *plus the Ancient Chinese Revealed.* New York: Clearbridge.

Wong, Ovid K. 1987. *Giant panda.* Chicago: Children's Press.

Wong, Ovid K., and Lam Ming-Long. 2007. *Using data analysis to improve learning toward 100% proficiency.* Lanham, MD: Rowman & Littlefield.

6

THE LEADER'S SELF-ASSESSMENT

In China, approximately 250 years before the period when Sun Tzu lived, was the period called Spring and Autumn. It was dominated by the philosophy of Confucius, a very prominent and well-respected teacher. His philosophy emphasized personal and governmental morality, correctness of social relationships, justice, and sincerity. The teachings of Confucius were recorded in a widely read essay titled the *Doctrine of the Mean* (*Chung Yung*). The Chinese title, *Chung Yung*, is composed of the elements "centrality" (*Chung*) and "normality" (*Yung*). The translation "The Mean" suggests the fundamental moral idea of moderation, balance, and suitableness. In this essay, the concept goes much deeper, denoting a basic norm of human action, which, if comprehended and complied with, will bring man and his actions into harmony with the universe. The essay was popular because the ideas represent philosophies not of the extreme right nor of the extreme left but in the middle (hence *the mean*), and many people are comfortable with the middle view of things. Many scholars, including political leaders, read the essay to guide their administration and to explore the profound meaning of life.

The *Doctrine of the Mean* includes a frequently quoted concept that teaches a person how to properly conduct himself or herself with reference to the family, the country, and the universe. It states that for a person to be successful and in harmony, he must first "discipline himself, before he can unite the family, then he can rule the country and finally he can conquer the universe." This life philosophy underscores the assessment and management of self. Next to the self is the family, and next to the family is the state or country. The essence of the philosophy points to the importance of self-discipline. It implies that without proper self-discipline, no major accomplishments will go further, to the family or to the country. In today's world, it is quite easy to understand the application of that ideal. Let us look at an example. One can ask, "How can an abusive father (self) possibly help his spouse and the children (family) to prosper?" One can also ask the subsequent question, "How can an abusive father possibly help to make contributions to the state (country)?"

Sun Tzu lived many years after Confucius. It is not surprising that Sun Tzu's wisdom was influenced by the philosophy of Confucius about the importance of self-knowing and self-assessment:

> Know yourself and know your enemy.
> You will be safe in every battle.
> You may know yourself but not know the enemy.
> You will then lose one battle for every one you win.
> You may not know yourself or the enemy.
> You will then lose every battle.
>
> (Gagliardi 2003, ch. 3)

Of all the quotes in the *Art of War*, this could be the most popular. It is used frequently even today in all walks of life. Sun Tzu asked the leader to assess his strengths and compare them to those of the enemy. An effective leader does not claim strengths or weaknesses until a through comparison to the enemy has been made. When the leader knows that his army is strong and his enemy is weak, he knows that his chance of victory is very high. Poor leadership is manifested when the leader does not know his strengths and those of the enemy. Obviously, there are different degrees of how well one knows oneself and the enemy.

Sun Tzu wrote that the degree of knowing oneself correlates to the chance of victory. Jonathan is a college graduate, and he is a strong student in terms of grade point average and good study habits. He wants to continue his education in the professional school of dentistry. He asked his father for advice about the dental school admission preparation, assuming that he was already well prepared academically. The father knew that his son was ready in terms of hard work and good grade point average; however, a crucial gatekeeper for admission was the dental admission test. He advised his son to take the mock dental admission examination to evaluate his readiness. Jonathan scored below average on his first attempt at the mock examination. If he had taken the real admission test, he would not have gained admission to the school of dentistry. Sun Tzu would say that Jonathan might be a good student; however, in terms of scoring high on the dental admission examination, he still did not know himself quite that well. The Jonathan story actually came to a happy ending. Jonathan studied very hard, and he became better acquainted with himself through many hours of study. He took numerous practice tests, until one day he went to his father and said, "I am ready now!" He knew the enemy (i.e., the dental admission examination); he also knew his strength regarding test readiness. Jonathan was accepted by seven dental schools. He is on his way to graduating from dental school, with the intention of going on for more training to become a root canal specialist.

SELF- AND OTHER AWARENESS ASSESSMENT IN LEADERSHIP

Education is a people business. Educators deal with students, parents, staff, faculty, fellow administrators, and other people in the school community. To be effective, a leader needs to know himself or herself and the people (i.e., the other) with whom he or she deals. To make the work relationship effective, a school leader needs to know about the organization, himself or herself as the organization's leader, and more important, what other people (i.e., the public) know about the organization and the organization's leader.

In the business of leadership, what is known to others is public perception. One veteran school superintendent admits that over 75 percent of his waking hours are spent giving the public the right perception of him and the school organization. He says that if information is known to him and to others, then it is open and public information. Large school organizations typically have a special person to convey school information, otherwise known as the public information officer. When school information is not handled correctly, it will give people an incorrect perception and image of the school, leading to unnecessary criticism and possibly a decrease in public support.

When information is known to the leader and not known to the public, it is hidden information. For example, as a rule the school administration does not openly discuss personnel issues in such public forums as meetings and publications. A person fired from a job can be given such reasons as personal matters, retirement, and other nonspecific causes.

When information is not known to both the leader and the public, the information is simply unknown. Unknown information does not concern the leader or the public, for the simple reason that nobody knows about it. Unknown information does not hurt the leader or the public and usually is of little or no concern to the school leader.

When information is not known to the leader but is known to the public, this is a blind spot of the leader. Many people see blind spots more as negatives, but that is not always true. If a school administrator shows empathetic behavior when meeting with people bringing concerns (but the administrator is not aware of this empathy), this is a positive blind spot. If another school administrator demonstrates passive aggressive behavior when meeting with people bringing concerns and that administrator is not aware of his or her hostility, this is a negative blind spot.

To be an effective leader, an administrator needs to know accurately what is public information, classified information, unknown information, and more important, blind information (a blind spot) for him or her and the organization. Table 6.1 shows a Johari matrix of how a leader might assess what is known to him or her and the public, as well as what is not known to them both, along with other known and unknown combinations. The matrix is a tool created by Joseph Luft and Harry Ingham in the 1950s to help people better understand themselves in relationship to other people. The Johari matrix is relevant to the current demand for and influence of leadership skills, behavior, cooperation, empathy, teamwork, and intergroup and interpersonal development. The Johari matrix has four quadrants. The first is information that is known to oneself and

Table 6.1.   Johari Matrix

	Known to Self	Unknown to Self
Known to Others	1. Open Area	2. Blind Area
Unknown to Others	3. Hidden Area	4. Unknown Area

to others. This is open and public information. The second is information that is known to others but not to oneself. This is blind information. The third quadrant is information that is known to oneself but not to others. This is hidden information. The fourth quadrant is information that is unknown to oneself and others. This is unknown information.

Let us look at how the Johari matrix is being used and applied in understanding oneself and others. Ada is a chief executive officer of a health organization. She is interested in better understanding herself and how other people in the organization see her. She follows the guidelines of the Johari procedure and picks five words, from a predetermined list of fifty-five adjectives (table 6.2), that she feels best describe her.

Ada picked confident, trustworthy, loving, self-assertive, and mature from the list. Do members of her executive team see her the same way? She does not know until she asks her team to describe her using the same list of adjectives. Ada has five members in her team. They follow the same procedure, each picking five adjectives that they feel best describe Ada. In general, the team picked confident, nervous, trustworthy, idealistic, and powerful as the best descriptors for Ada. Finally, Ada categorized the adjectives and placed them into the four quadrants of the Johari matrix (table 6.3).

Table 6.2.   The Fifty-Five Adjectives

Able	Accepting	Adaptable	Bold	Brave
Calm	Caring	Cheerful	Clever	Complex
Confident	Dependable	Dignified	Energetic	Extroverted
Friendly	Giving	Happy	Helpful	Idealistic
Independent	Ingenious	Intelligent	Introverted	Kind
Knowledgeable	Logical	Loving	Mature	Modest
Nervous	Observant	Organized	Patient	Powerful
Proud	Quiet	Reflective	Relaxed	Religious
Responsive	Searching	Self-assertive	Self-conscious	Sensible
Sentimental	Shy	Silly	Spontaneous	Sympathetic
Tense	Trustworthy	Warm	Wise	Witty

Table 6.3. Ada's Johari Matrix

	Known to Self	Unknown to Self
Known to Others	confident, trustworthy	nervous, idealistic, powerful
Unknown to Others	loving, self-assertive, mature	able, calm, friendly, independent, knowledgeable, proud, responsive, sentimental, tense, accepting, caring, dependable, giving, ingenious, logical, observant, quiet, searching, shy, adaptable, cheerful, dignified, happy, intelligent, organized, reflective, silly, warm, bold, clever, energetic, helpful, introverted, patient, relaxed, self conscious, spontaneous, wise, brave, complex, extroverted, kind, modest, religious, sensible, sympathetic, witty.

Once the descriptors have been categorized, the interpretation is quite straightforward. Ada is confident and trustworthy. These qualities are known to herself and her colleagues. Ada is loving, self-assertive, and mature. These qualities are known only to herself and not to others. What that means is that these are the hidden qualities that Ada did not get to show to the public. If loving, for example, is important for Ada to relate to her colleagues, then she needs to reveal it more vividly in her work behaviors. The qualities that are not known to Ada and to her colleagues are not important at this point, because additional qualities will be disclosed in the future through work relationships. Of concern to Ada are the qualities in the third quadrant of the matrix. Ada's colleagues perceive her as nervous, idealistic, and powerful; these qualities are not known to her at all. Ada took note of the information because being nervous, idealistic, and powerful are her blind spots. As the CEO of the organization, it is imperative that she correct these deficiencies if they are negative to her leadership and the well-being of the organization.

Let us now look at a Johari matrix for John (table 6.4), a recent hire who is new to the existing administrative team headed by Ada. Without going through the Johari exercise details, the open area is small, because other people know little about the new person. Similarly, the blind area is small (2) for the same reason. The hidden or avoided issues and feelings are a relatively large area. In this particular example, the unknown area is the largest because John is young and lacks self-knowledge.

Table 6.4. John's Johari Matrix

1 Open area	2 Blind area
Hidden area 3	Unknown area 4

Table 6.5. Camy's Johari Matrix

1 Open area	2 Blind area
Hidden area 3	Unknown area 4

Next, let us study the Johari matrix of Camy (table 6.5). Camy is an established member of the same administrative team headed by Ada. Compared to John's, her open region is large because the administrative team (i.e., others) knows a lot about Camy that she also knows. Through the processes of disclosure and receiving feedback, the open area has expanded; at the same time, the blind and unknown areas have been reduced.

As the leader of a school organization, one can encourage the use of the Johari matrix to better understand people and their working relationships. Information in the matrix can optimize people's behavior toward the advancement of the organization.

LEARNING STYLE ASSESSMENT

People in leadership positions are both learners and teachers. A new leader in an organization might first learn about the existing workplace culture, including the people, policies, and procedures before tweaking and leading in a new direction for organizational improvement. As a leader, how does one learn? As a leader, how does one teach? The answers are closely related, because how a person learns is also related to how he or she teaches. When communication is at a premium in a forward-moving organization, the learning and teaching style of the leader is pivotal. As the leader of an organization, do you know your learning style so you can communicate effectively with members of your organization? Who are the learners? They are different in age, appearance, likes and dislikes, background and experience, and most important, the ability to learn.

Learning style analysts differentiate three kinds of learners: visual, auditory, and tactile. Visual learners use charts, maps, filmstrips, notes, videos, and other visual materials to help them learn. They learn by the visualization of information. They work best when they can see the big picture of things. Visual learners like to write meeting notes so they can visually review what happened. They learn by seeing. Auditory learners are listeners. They prefer taped lecture notes over written notes. They also like to read, summarize, and recite to enhance understanding. Auditory learners prefer to talk to other students about class materials and discuss the information given. Auditory learners learn by listening. Tactile learners are hands-on students. They might trace words as one is saying them, and taking lecture notes is very important to them. Tactile learners also like to associate what they learn with real-world things or occurrences. They role play when it is appropriate. They ask the teacher to show them how to do something instead of telling them how to do it. Tactile learners learn by doing.

In the real world, workers have a combination of learning styles. A person might be a hybrid of 60 percent visual learner and 40 percent auditory learner. Rarely will one find a person who is 100 percent one kind of learner, because learning is usually better when one uses more than one sense. Many people claim that they prefer a predominant learning style.

Study and respond to the twenty-four statements about learning in table 6.6. For each statement there is a choice of *often* (6 points), *sometimes* (4 points), and *seldom* (2 points). Place the point value on the line next to the corresponding statement. When you are done with all the responses, add up the points in each column to obtain the total score under each heading (see table 6.7). Are you predominantly a visual learner, an auditory learner, or a tactile learner?

An effective leader is cognizant of his or her learning style as well as the learning styles of coworkers. This is similar to Sun Tzu's strategy of knowing oneself and others. The leader may need to adjust his or her dominant mode from time to time to accommodate the learning styles of the staff. To understand one's learning style is one thing, and an inability to adjust could be detrimental to effective communication and the well-being of the organization. In your school learning community,

Table 6.6. Learning Style Inventory

	Often	Sometimes	Seldom
1. I learn best by listening to a presentation that includes information, explanation, and discussion.			
2. I learn best by scanning written information on a board, a piece of poster paper, or other visual aids followed by reading from a book.			
3. I learn best by writing down the information for subsequent visual review.			
4. I learn best by using posters, models, or hands-on practice activities.			
5. I understand when explanations are shown using diagrams and flow charts.			
6. I learn how the brakes of a bicycle work by taking the bike apart and then putting it back together again.			
7. I always make graphs and charts in my PowerPoint presentations.			
8. I can tell even the subtle difference of sounds when they are presented in pairs.			
9. I can easily drive from A to B by writing down the road directions down several times.			
10. I can easily drive from A to B by following directions on a map.			
11. I usually get good grades in class by listening to lectures.			
12. When thinking hard, I twirl pens or pencils with my fingers.			
13. I prefer to spell a new word by repeating the word out loud rather than by writing it down.			
14. To get the same piece of information, I prefer reading a newspaper article to listening to a radio report.			
15. I like to chew gum or snack when I study for an examination.			
16. I like to form a picture in my head before I start sharing an idea with friends.			
17. I explain a multistep procedure best by using my fingers.			
18. I enjoy listening to a good speech rather than reading the same information in a newspaper.			

	Often	Sometimes	Seldom
19. I enjoy working with jigsaw puzzles.			
20. I twiddle objects in my fingers when I solve a mathematics equation.			
21. I prefer listening to the radio rather than reading the world news in the newspaper.			
22. I prefer learning information about the impact of global warming by reading about it.			
23. I feel very much at ease by communicating my feelings by hugging and handshaking.			
24. I prefer oral directions over written directions.			

do you prefer to use lecture, discussion group, role-playing, brainstorming, symposium, or some other method of learning and teaching? What are your reasons for choosing that method(s)?

One school leader presents a professional training workshop at a state teacher conference. At the beginning of the workshop, he asks each participant to draw a shape on a blank piece of paper that best represents him or her. There are four shape choices: a circle, a triangle, a square, and a wavy line. The workshop participants think for a moment and swiftly draw the shapes of their choice. The workshop leader

Table 6.7.   Learning Style Score Tally

Visual		Auditory		Tactile	
Number	Points	Number	Points	Number	Points
2		1		4	
3		5		6	
7		8		9	
10		11		12	
14		13		15	
16		18		17	
19		21		20	
22		24		23	
Total		Total		Total	

then asks people drawing the circle, the triangle, the square, and the wavy line to raise their hands in turn. The distribution of the circles, the triangles, and the squares is about equal. The smallest group of people is the wavy line. The leader then asks the participants to divide into four activity groups so that each is a good mix of all the shapes. He explains that the circles are people who avoid conflicts, the triangles are people who often ask "what is the point" in a conversation or discussion, the squares are people who like to see things tidy and organized, and the wavy lines are creative and like to think out of the box. The workshop participants get a good laugh out of this ice-breaking activity; however, they also see a connection between the activity and the real work world. In the real work world, we all have to deal with people with different operational styles. These people are the circles, the triangles, the squares, and the wavy lines.

LEADERSHIP SELF-ASSESSMENT

The purpose of the self-survey is to establish a starting point to use in the process of becoming or remaining an effective leader. The questions are actually statements asking for responses to a situation. The statements are designed purely to help you reflect, and there is no absolute right or wrong answer. The recipe for a successful leader, according to Sun Tzu, starts with the philosophy of the leader, followed by leadership traits, methods of delivery, and the execution of the plan in harmony with the environment. Do your leadership skills measure up to the challenge? You will find out by taking the leadership self-survey in table 6.8.

There are 100 items in this leadership survey. Circle your responses as follows: (1) represents *No Opinion*, (2) represents *Do Not Agree*, and (3) represents *Agree*.

What is your total score from the survey? Use the score guide in table 6.9 and reference it to Sun Tzu's standards.

An aspiring young man entered the field of educational administration with advanced formal training, a few years of successful classroom teaching, and several university and professional organization awards. His early experience in school administration did not come from books. Books did not show him how to supervise the lunchroom and the play-

Table 6.8. Leadership Survey

1. The job of a school leader is mostly about relationships with people.	(1)	(2)	(3)
2. The teacher reviewed with her class the plan to take a field trip to the Museum of Science and Technology.	(1)	(2)	(3)
3. José found a wallet left behind in a restaurant. He picked it up and gave to the restaurant manager.	(1)	(2)	(3)
4. You are the commander of an army. You lead your troops to war to protect your country.	(1)	(2)	(3)
5. An elementary school principal recommended to release a teacher because his students failed.	(1)	(2)	(3)
6. Dr. Jones reorganized the teaching assignment of the department based on the expertise of the teachers.	(1)	(2)	(3)
7. The superintendent shared with her staff why the schools needed a tax referendum for education.	(1)	(2)	(3)
8. Due to resource constraints, math is selected over science for student improvement.	(1)	(2)	(3)
9. To clarify a talking point in a committee meeting you paraphrase the idea of a discussion.	(1)	(2)	(3)
10. As a supervisor, it is best to reveal your plan with your workers before it is implemented.	(1)	(2)	(3)
11. The superintendent met with a board committee before discussing an issue at the board meeting.	(1)	(2)	(3)
12. Rosa drove on a highway and saw a car on the side of the road in an accident. She stopped the car and helped.	(1)	(2)	(3)
13. Angelee pursued a career in administration because she felt she could better serve the needs of students.	(1)	(2)	(3)
14. Abigail is a tenured teacher. She was asked to retire early because 75% of her students failed 3 years in a row.	(1)	(2)	(3
15. A school has a meager budget. The principal allocated 80% of that budget for the teaching staff.	(1)	(2)	(3)
16. A principal opens up the school auditorium for regular community activities.	(1)	(2)	(3)
17. A school administrator invites local business people to regular school community meetings to share his vision.	(1)	(2)	(3)
18. The school board approves conference requests based on the mission and the current school improvement needs.	(1)	(2)	(3)
19. The goals for improving student achievement is based on an 8.5% increase from the achievement base line.	(1)	(2)	(3)
20. Due to resource constraints, English language arts is selected over science for student improvement.	(1)	(2)	(3)
21. Students exceeded the math state learning standards. The school passed the No Child Left Behind law.	(1)	(2)	(3)
22. The administrator often takes risks to benefit the well being of the school and students.	(1)	(2)	(3)
23. The department chair rotates the teaching schedule to familiarize her staff with the different level courses.	(1)	(2)	(3)
24. When you failed a task you always try again using a different strategy.	(1)	(2)	(3)

(continues)

Table 6.8. *(continued)*

25. Veronica always encourages her staff to take calculated risks but to avoid making unaffordable mistakes.	(1)	(2)	(3)
26. School decisions are best made based on what is good for the students.	(1)	(2)	(3)
27. Nathaniel forgoes his family vacation to Hawaii to complete his end of the year report.	(1)	(2)	(3)
28. Your subordinate calls in sick and you figure out how the missing work can be covered in the office.	(1)	(2)	(3)
29. A co-worker had difficulty in completing his work. You step in to help the coworker personally.	(1)	(2)	(3)
30. You pride yourself because people often come to you for help.	(1)	(2)	(3)
31. Someone in the office picked an argument with you. You resolve the argument with patience.	(1)	(2)	(3
32. As an administrator, you have no problem in telling your workers that they make mistakes at work.	(1)	(2)	(3)
33. You feel comfortable speaking in front of a group in various settings.	(1)	(2)	(3)
34. You can respond to questions whether or not you know the answer.	(1)	(2)	(3)
35. You can return phone calls and e-mail messages within 48 hours.	(1)	(2)	(3)
36. Due to resource constraints, science is selected over social studies for student improvement.	(1)	(2)	(3)
37. Many bad decisions are made because they are based on the specific interests of the adults.	(1)	(2)	(3)
38. The athletic director asked for a bonus after his school won the state basketball championship.	(1)	(2)	(3)
39. You are comfortable to share your success story with both your colleagues and strangers.	(1)	(2)	(3)
40. You take time out of your busy schedule to visit classrooms and other student activities.	(1)	(2)	(3)
41. You are not threatened when surrounded by people who know more than you.	(1)	(2)	(3)
42. People in the office come to your for advice on work that they do not know what to do.	(1)	(2)	(3)
43. You are able to change plan at moment's notice.	(1)	(2)	(3)
44. You enjoy walking your dog in the park after dinner.	(1)	(2)	(3)
45. You keep up with your professional reading as often as you can afford time.	(1)	(2)	(3)
46. You make decisions based on mostly what you know yourself and what other people tell you.	(1)	(2)	(3)
47. People in the office would come to you for advice on personal matters.	(1)	(2)	(3)
48. You are able to tackle several tasks at one time without being over stressed.	(1)	(2)	(3)
49. You keep up with professional development activities to stay sharp in your field.	(1)	(2)	(3)
50. Your staff know the intricate operations of your office because they are cross-trained.	(1)	(2)	(3)
51. Jerry gave Joan first a verbal, then written warning, and finally a write-up for excessive unexcused absences.	(1)	(2)	(3)

52. You rely on phone, email, memo, and meetings to communicate   (1) (2) (3)
    with staff.
53. Jeannie found out the learning style of her staff and aligns her   (1) (2) (3)
    presentation style with that learning style.
54. You feel comfortable when people around you give you constructive   (1) (2) (3)
    advice.
55. In hiring teaching staff, certification is more important than experience   (1) (2) (3)
    and formal training combined.
56. Jose talked to the office managers and used the information to   (1) (2) (3)
    formulate the office meeting agenda.
57. As the chief executive officer of a school district, David always hides   (1) (2) (3)
    his emotion well in the public.
58. The school business manager did not approve a board expense   (1) (2) (3)
    reimbursement without receipts.
59. Rhonda, a school principal, did not question Ada, a teacher, for taking   (1) (2) (3)
    her personal day.
60. A school improvement team set a 9% math student achievement goal   (1) (2) (3)
    for the new school year.
61. Differentiated instruction is selected over mental mathematics as the   (1) (2) (3)
    theme of a school conference.
62. As a meeting chair, you regularly bring people back to the main   (1) (2) (3)
    meeting agenda.
63. For office productivity, staff attitude is more important than skills   (1) (2) (3)
    and knowledge.
64. A principal hired a teacher with 5 years of experience because of   (1) (2) (3)
    cost and experience flexibility.
65. After getting top scores in the state test, the school principal   (1) (2) (3)
    suggested a school tax referendum increase.
66. A computer lab manager placed all the computer stations with the   (1) (2) (3)
    monitor screens facing the middle of the room.
67. An improvement goal for finding the average in math is selected over   (1) (2) (3)
    an improvement goal for statistics.
68. "Every child can learn" is not the same as "every child can learn   (1) (2) (3)
    to his potential."
69. Your colleagues give you constructive criticism about the politics   (1) (2) (3)
    of the work place.
70. To believe that every student can learn is more important to a teacher   (1) (2) (3)
    than good home–school relationship.
71. To believe that every student can learn is more important to a teacher   (1) (2) (3)
    than frequently testing the students.
72. The academic achievement of a school is as important as the athletic   (1) (2) (3)
    achievement.
73. Everything being equal, a school principal hires teachers to match the   (1) (2) (3)
    ethnic composition of the students.
74. To schedule the graduation ceremony the same evening as the school   (1) (2) (3)
    board meeting is poor planning.
75. A school principal recommends a lower pupil–teacher ratio for the   (1) (2) (3)
    primary grades and not the higher grades.

(continues)

Table 6.8. Leadership Survey

76. A superintendent always gets to know citizen concerns before they go to the public school board meeting.	(1)	(2)	(3)
77. You enjoy going to work because you get along well with your superior and your subordinates.	(1)	(2)	(3)
78. You are not hesitant to ask your supervisor for a word of advice.	(1)	(2)	(3)
79. As a manager, you take time to talk to people about their family, interests and aspirations.	(1)	(2)	(3)
80. Under your management, your staff is not afraid to take calculated risks.	(1)	(2)	(3)
81. You mediate a dispute by listening to both sides before collaboratively come to a solution.	(1)	(2)	(3)
82. You are not hesitant to discipline your staff for lying about their sick days.	(1)	(2)	(3)
83. You do not feel lonely for holding the very top position of your organization.	(1)	(2)	(3)
84. You are not defensive when someone points out a view that is different from yours.	(1)	(2)	(3)
85. You pay the restaurant bill when a small group of your office staff eats out to celebrate the success of your school.	(1)	(2)	(3)
86. You always make the expectation clear to your staff before you hold them accountable.	(1)	(2)	(3)
87. In doing the elementary school class schedule, you put reading in the morning and science in the afternoon.	(1)	(2)	(3)
88. Given the choice, you prefer not to house students from kindergarten through eighth grade in the same building.	(1)	(2)	(3)
89. In staff evaluation, work habit, personality and work performance may not be related.	(1)	(2)	(3)
90. You do not call a staff member about work when he is on vacation.	(1)	(2)	(3)
91. You enforce the same standards of performance on you and your staff.	(1)	(2)	(3)
92. You set a deadline for an evaluation report and you do not accept anything coming in late.	(1)	(2)	(3)
93. You portray a similar personality at work at home and at play.	(1)	(2)	(3)
94. You are efficient in doing one task or several other tasks at the same time.	(1)	(2)	(3)
95. As a supervisor you take time to share with your staff about your family and favorite pastime.	(1)	(2)	(3)
96. You do not feel threatened when your subordinate holds a private meeting with your boss.	(1)	(2)	(3)
97. You prefer to hire people to work for you and with more formal training and experience than you.	(1)	(2)	(3)
98. You prefer not to put the freshmen students in the same wing of the building as the senior students.	(1)	(2)	(3)
99. Teaching to the state test is teaching to the state learning standards.	(1)	(2)	(3)
100. Mr. Fernando's reading class had 80% failure. The teacher is mostly responsible for the student failure.	(1)	(2)	(3)

Table 6.9.   Leadership Score Guide

Score Range	What It Means
Under 150	Does not meet Sun Tzu's standards
151–225	Meets Sun Tzu's standards
226–289	Exceeds Sun Tzu's standards
290–300	You are Sun Tzu's equal!

ground when he served as an elementary school principal. Professors did not teach him how to tackle intricate workplace politics when he served in various other school administrative positions. Everything else he needed to know about effective school leadership he learned on the job. A person might score high in a leadership survey, but that does not automatically make him or her a supreme school commander. What you learn from a book is head knowledge. That knowledge somehow has to be effectively executed and seamlessly blended with your own personality. One important thing veteran administrators have learned in various school administrative jobs is that the leader is pivotal in setting the climate of the workplace. The leader can lead by his or her position; in that case, subordinates follow the leader mostly out of fear and with little respect. On the other hand, the leader can lead by example; in that case subordinates follow the leader out of respect and loyalty to the organization. The yin and yang of school leadership is unique in that an effective leader sometimes needs to be feared and at other times needs to be respected.

Is it possible for a person to be a loving father and husband at home and a fearless school superintendent of a district with 6,000 students? The answer is, anything is possible. However, it is almost like saying that as soon as the father leaves home to go to work he has to change his personality drastically to meet the demands of the school district. To perform well in one's personal life and at work, does one need to have a split personality, like Dr. Jekyll and Mr. Hyde? Wouldn't it be nice if the same personality and behavior traits could apply to being a loving parent and spouse and a fearless school superintendent? Many school administrators feel frustrated or even defeated because they are not able to transition their personality effectively from home or personal life to work and be emotionally detached. Sun Tzu would advise them to accurately assess their selves and the tasks that they are up against to avoid disappointment; to know oneself and the enemy will keep one safe in every battle.

REFERENCE

Gagliardi, Gary. 2003. *The* Art of War *plus the Ancient Chinese Revealed.* New York: Clearbridge.

7

TURNING SUN TZU'S
WISDOM INTO ACTIONS

A CONCEPT MAP OF SUN TZU'S STRATEGIES

The *Art of War* is a plethora of strategies from Sun Tzu. Scholars spend years studying the strategies and apply them to solving real-world situations. In this book, thirty-three quotes from Sun Tzu are used. Figure 7.1 is a concept map of the strategies described in those quotes.

A concept map is a diagram showing the relationships among concepts. Concepts are connected with arrows, in a downward-branching, hierarchical structure. The concepts at the top are typically broad, general, and inclusive. Concepts at the bottom are narrow, specific, and less inclusive. As a rule, the narrow concepts are subsumed under the general concepts in the map. Figure 7.1 has the leader at the very top, represented by Abraham Lincoln, the sixteenth president of the United States. The president has the pivotal role in leading the country to success and prosperity. What is guiding the thinking and behavior of the leader is his behind-the-scenes philosophy and moral purpose. President Lincoln introduced measures that resulted in the abolition of slavery and issued the Emancipation Proclamation. He is well known for ending slavery in the United States, holding close to his heart that all people are created equal, and that is his moral purpose. What is of value

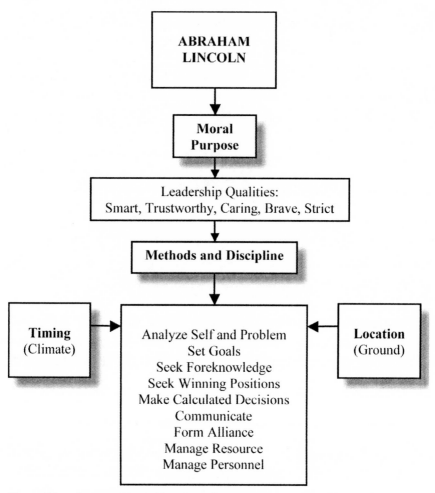

Figure 7.1.   Concept Map of Sun Tzu's Strategies

to him and what is of no value to him affects his decisions and dealings with people, as well as the fate of the country.

In education, will the school leader champion the organization, the students, or personal gain? This is the crucial decision the leader has to make based on his or her moral purpose. An effective leader has many fine yet difficult-to-measure qualities, such as being smart, trustworthy, caring, brave, and strict. These qualities are highly influenced and shaped by the ultimate moral purpose that resides in the leader. For example, the school leader might be brave risk taker, but is he taking risks at the expense of the students, the organization, or himself?

Methods of executing a leader's responsibilities include a wide range of internal and external behaviors. If methods and discipline make up the tool box, then the methods of execution, such as analyzing oneself and the problem or setting goals, are the tools. An experienced leader will have many tools in the box and will select the right one to get the job done. A unique feature of the concept map that reflects Sun Tzu's philosophy is the influence of timing and location on the effectiveness of the method of execution. According to Sun Tzu's wisdom, the successful execution of methods and discipline is supported by the right timing and location, which are not always under the control of the leader.

APPLYING KNOWLEDGE OF STRENGTHS AND WEAKNESSES FOR IMPROVEMENT

"When you form your strategy, know the strengths and weaknesses of your plan."

> Manage your military position like water.
> Water takes every shape.
> It avoids the high and moves to the low.
> Your war can take any shape.
> It must avoid the strong and strike the weak.
> Water follows the shape of the land that directs its flow.
> Your forces follow the enemy, who determines how you win.
>
> (Gagliardi 2003, ch. 6)

Weakness and strength is a major subject discussed in the *Art of War* because understanding them helps the leader to compare his army to the enemy's. Ultimately, the leader uses the comparison to calculate the winning position, foil the plan of the enemy, to disrupt alliances, attack the opposing army, or storm a fortified city wall. Sun Tzu's supreme battle strategy is still and always to win by not fighting, as in foiling the plan of the enemy. The development of the weakness and strength precept is briefly described in chapter 1. (Sun Tzu observed and took notes on the behavior of the running water after a heavy rainstorm.)

Let us return to the application of understanding strengths and weaknesses to improving education. As a leader, what is your goal for improvement? We need to be clear that improvement efforts must bring ultimate student success regardless of whether the efforts are direct or indirect. Under the current regulation of the No Child Left Behind Act, student success for the most part means academic performance in the core subject areas (e.g., reading, mathematics). Figure 7.2 describes the support variables for student success.

In figures 7.1 and 7.2, one leader is shown at the top and the other at the bottom. There is no absolute right or wrong in either leadership configuration; the leader himself has to feel comfortable with and be effective in how he or she leads and supports the organization for success.

Rose Hill is a performing suburban public elementary (K–6) school with a total enrollment of 652 students. The student population is 60 percent white, 0.5 percent black, 5.2 percent Hispanic, 28 percent Asian/Pacific Islander, 2.7 percent Native American, and 3.6 percent multiracial/ethnic. The No Child Left Behind Act requires this specific breakdown for reporting purposes. Under the law, student success is measured by the success of the individual disaggregated student groups, not the average of the whole aggregated student body. The Rose Hill student population has 8.3 percent low-income students, 12.6 percent Limited English Proficient (LEP) students, a 0 percent chronic truancy rate, a 3.0 percent mobility rate, and finally, an attendance rate of 98.2 percent. This information is not a contributing factor to academic performance, although education researchers believe that the percentage of low-income students is likely to be a significant contributing factor to student performance.

Under the guidance of the leadership team, four school variables were examined and analyzed to understand the strengths and weaknesses of student academic performance at Rose Hill. The four factors were instructional setting, school resources, teacher quality, and professional development (see figure 7.2). Dr. Hassan is the principal and leader of the Rose Hill administrative team. Over the summer break, she called the leadership team together for a three-day data retreat. The

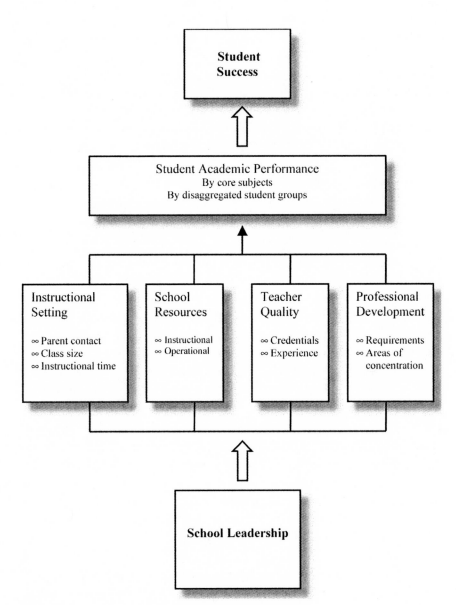

Figure 7.2. Support Variables for Student Success

purpose of the retreat was to analyze the school data and propose a plan of improvement for the new school year.

The first variable the administrative team studied was the student academic performance report card (see table 7.1). The report card showed the percentages of student scores in each of the four performance categories. State and federal laws require public school districts to release report cards to the public each year. The reports include percentage of state test scores categorized in four categories: Level I (Academic Warning), Level II (Below Standards), Level III (Meets Standards), and Level IV (Exceeds Standards). Level I student work demonstrates limited knowledge and skills mastery in the subject, and because of major learning gaps, students apply knowledge and skills ineffectively. Level II student work demonstrates basic knowledge and skills mastery in the subject. However, because of learning gaps, students apply knowledge and skills in limited ways. Level III student work demonstrates proficient knowledge and skills mastery in the subject. Students effectively apply knowledge and skills to solve problems. Level IV student work demonstrates advanced knowledge and skills mastery in the subject. Students creatively apply knowledge and skills to solve problems and evaluate the results. The report card showed the performance of nine student groups: all (all the student groups combined), white, black, Hispanic, Asian/Pacific Islander, Native American, multiracial/ethnic, special education (disabilities), and low income (economically disadvantaged).

The Rose Hill administrative team analyzed the data and came to the following conclusions regarding strengths and weaknesses of student performance. With reference to reading and mathematics, reading achievement was stronger than math in both grades 3 and 5. Reading, however, showed a larger decrease in student achievement score than did math, from grade 3 to grade 5. In terms of the student subgroups, white, Asian, and multiracial students outperformed the other groups in reading and math in both grades 3 and 5. Hispanic, special education, and low-income students consistently underperformed. For improvement planning, it is obvious that Rose Hill needs to decrease the percentage of Level I and II students and increase the percentage of Level III and IV students in reading and mathematics. The percentage changes must reflect uniformly across all the student subgroups. How will factors like instructional setting, school resources, teacher quality,

Table 7.1. Student Performance Summary

		Grade 3						
	Reading				Math			
	I	II	III	IV	I	II	III	IV
ALL	0.00	4.00	39.00	57.00	10.00	12.00	45.60	32.40
White	0.00	4.00	37.50	58.50	9.80	4.75	76.80	8.65
Black	1.20	18.70	30.10	50.00	1.80	45.79	49.60	2.81
Hispanic	3.40	40.60	31.00	25.00	7.56	28.70	58.60	5.14
Asian	0.00	0.00	50.00	50.00	0.00	15.80	43.00	41.20
Native A.	5.00	35.00	50.00	10.00	0.86	26.20	45.12	27.82
Multi Racial	0.00	0.00	47.20	52.80	0.80	20.30	66.20	12.70
Sp. Ed.	20.70	12.65	33.35	33.30	24.89	30.87	30.00	14.24
Low Income	31.00	40.00	27.00	2.00	20.00	40.00	38.00	2.00

		Grade 5						
	Reading				Math			
	I	II	III	IV	I	II	III	IV
ALL	0.00	20.50	49.60	29.90	12.34	15.00	40.84	31.82
White	1.20	12.00	34.00	52.80	11.00	15.00	43.80	30.20
Black	5.70	24.90	30.70	38.70	2.80	50.00	44.60	2.60
Hispanic	5.93	50.10	32.00	11.97	12.00	34.00	37.00	17.00
Asian	0.00	0.00	54.00	46.00	0.00	18.00	45.00	37.00
Native A.	0.50	14.82	46.00	38.68	1.20	30.00	42.00	26.80
Multi Racial	0.00	20.00	45.00	35.00	0.60	20.00	68.00	11.40
Sp. Ed.	30.00	28.00	40.00	2.00	30.00	35.10	23.00	11.90
Low Income	24.00	30.00	37.90	8.10	21.00	42.00	32.00	5.00

Legend:
I   Academic Warning
II Below Standards
III Meets Standards
IV Exceeds Standards

and professional development affect the proposed Rose Hill student improvement plan? These factors are examined below.

The second variable the administrative team studied was information about the instructional setting. Instructional setting includes parent contacts, student-to-teacher ratio (class size), and time devoted to teaching the core subjects (e.g., reading and mathematics). The data record indicated that the school had 95 percent parent contacts. Parent contacts can be parent response to school activities, e-mail, or phone messages. Rose Hill has strong parent or home support. Parent support is considered to be a strength. The average class size ranged from fifteen in the lower grades to twenty in the upper grades. The class size is also considered to be a strength, as the pupil–teacher ratio is low compared to the state average of twenty for the lower grades and twenty-five for the higher grades. How about the time devoted to teaching the core subjects? Per day, students spend 150 minutes on English/language arts, 50 minutes on mathematics, 30 minutes on science, and 30 minutes on social science. Is the instructional time adequate? Based on the strengths and weaknesses of the student performance report card data, how should Rose Hill adjust the instructional setting to achieve higher student performance? What are the factors affecting the adjustment of the instructional setting?

The third variable the team studied was school resources. School resources for the most part are financial matters. The question that one needs to answer in this area is whether the school has enough money to support the students in terms of learning and school operation. It is obvious that learning expenditure has a direct impact on student learning, because the money pays for the teachers, the support staff, and the instructional materials. The operating costs, on the other hand, pay for indirect costs not dealing with instruction. Noninstructional expenditures include school maintenance, rent, insurance, and utilities. Rose Hill had an instructional per pupil expenditure of $7,000 and an operating cost per pupil of $9,000. Its financial status was considered average, as it was comparable to the average state figures. School budget preparation and the regulation of expenditures can pose challenges for any school leader because they are be impacted by the climate (timing) and ground (location) factors pointed out by Sun Tzu. What is the likelihood that a school can raise its revenues (through property tax) when 85 percent of students are from low-income families or the majority of the residents in the school community are on fixed incomes? Sun Tzu would call this a ground factor. What is the likelihood that a school can raise its revenues (through a tax referendum) when the community just passed a referendum two years ago? Sun Tzu would all this a climate factor. (The preparation of a school budget was discussed in chapter 3 under activity-based budgeting.) Based on the strengths and weaknesses of the student performance report card data, how should Rose Hill plan to use its resources to achieve higher student performance? What are the factors affecting the adjustment of the instructional and operational budget?

Last but not least, the school team collected and analyzed information about teacher quality. Teacher quality is obviously very important to the improvement of student performance because the teacher is the lifeline of the student learning process. The human resource department gave the administrative team a report showing that the majority of the teaching staff was white female and that 60 percent of the teachers had master's degrees and above. Nine percent of the teachers had emergency or provisional credentials, while the remainder were highly qualified teachers. The No Child Left Behind Act requires that teachers be highly qualified, and they should not teach in areas outside their credentials. Before the scrutiny of the law, there were teachers instructing outside their certified areas. As measured against the law, Rose Hill needs to reduce the percent of provisional teachers to 0. Teacher quality is considered a weakness. Based on the strengths and weaknesses of the student performance report card data, how should Rose Hill plan the hiring of new teachers to achieve higher student performance? What are the factors affecting the hiring of highly qualified new teachers?

Closely related to teacher quality is the plan for professional development. How will Rose Hill sustain and improve the quality of teachers so they can do their best in teaching the students? The professional development records indicated that 65 percent of the teachers attended English language arts meetings and conferences; 10 percent of the teachers attended mathematics conferences; and the remaining 25 percent attended science, social science, music, physical education, and technology conferences. Again, based on the strengths and weaknesses of the student performance report card data, how should Rose Hill develop and align an effective professional development plan to enhance higher student performance? What are the factors affecting the development of a professional development plan?

TURNING THEORY INTO ACTION

Theory without action is a daydream
Action without theory is a nightmare.

Chinese proverb

Every year, thousands and thousands of educators congregate in various convention centers around the nation to discuss and share their theories, only to return home a few days later to do what they do more or less the same way they did before the convention. Why?

There are two major reasons. First, changes in education are generally introduced in a very convoluted way before they reach the teachers. People and systems are resistant to change, and education is conservative about its basic modus operandi. In 1983, the quality of American education was examined in *A Nation at Risk*. The report described the deep-rooted problems facing American schools. In 1994, the Goals 2000: Educate America Act was passed by the U.S. Congress to improve schools by setting national goals. In 2001, the requirements of No Child Left Behind became law to develop and enforce schoolwide accountability focusing on student achievement. It took the country eleven years to set improvement goals after defining problems, and another seven years to enforce accountability. In other words, it took the American education system eighteen long and convoluted years to define problems, set goals, and enforce accountability! If people and the education system are not slow to change, then what is?

The second reason theories are not turned immediately into action by educational leaders is that they are too busy to reflect on and implement such theories. This may be an excuse for many, but professional developers claim that if an idea is learned (e.g., from a meeting or convention) but not used within a week, that idea is not likely to ever be used. Leaders often fail to recognize important trends and identify needed changes because they are too bogged down in day-to-day operations of the workplace, and they literally cannot see the forest for the trees. Leaders must be able to strategically view the environment as if they were on a terrace. One of the requirements of viewing the environment from the terrace is to see the field of action from a different perspective and yet not to create a dissonance between the leader and the field of action. There is a delicate balance between the leader and the field of action, and if the leader is too far removed from the field (e.g., taking the view from the tenth floor), a disconnect will be created. The terrace view of the environment requires that the leader step back and take the time and space to see what is happening, with purposeful reflection and self-assessment.

Learning is defined as a change in behavior over time. Educators compare the pre- and post-test achievement of students to show evidence of learning. If there is no difference between the pre- and post-test performance, according to many educators, learning did not take place, and there were no educational gains. Leadership training is similar, in that if the knowledge and skills learned are not applied, then what has been learned is not internalized, and in time it will diminish. The *Interstate School Leaders Licensure Consortium: Standards for School Leaders* and the *Skills for Successful 21st Century School Leaders: Standards for Peak Performers* use such action verbs as promote, facilitate, understand, respond, collaborate, mobilize, ensure, advocate, nurture, sustain, create, build, make, show, plan, use, evaluate, enhance, and demonstrate to define standards for school leaders.

In the first chapter of this book we discussed the relevance of Sun Tzu. In this last chapter we go full circle to talk about applying Sun Tzu's theory to actions, thus reinforcing the connection of Sun Tzu's wisdom in the real work world. Table 7.2 is a summary of the thirty-three quotes from Sun Tzu referenced in this book. The first three columns list the chapter, the quotation, and the main idea of the quotation. In the fourth column you should list an action plan in response to the question, "How might I apply this?" It is obvious that different people will use the application differently, so what goes in the action reflection column will vary. We are confident that careful reflection through action planning can make Sun Tzu's wisdom relevant and purposeful to your area of work in education. It is further hoped that this reflective learning activity can create internal growth that leads to effective external leadership behaviors.

REFERENCES

Council of Chief State School Officers. 1996. *Interstate School Leaders Licensure Consortium: Standards for school leaders.* Washington, DC: Authors.

Gagliardi, Gary. 2003. *The* Art of War *plus the Ancient Chinese Revealed.* New York: Clearbridge.

Hoyle, J. R, F. W. English, and B. E. Steffy. 1998. *Skills for successful 21st century school leaders: Standards for peak performers.* Arlington, VA: American Association of School Administrators.

Table 7.2. Action Reflection from Sun Tzu's Quotes

Chapter	Sun Tzu's Quote	Concept	Action Reflection
2	Your skills (as a leader) come from five factors. Study these factors when you plan war. You must insist on knowing your situation. Discuss the philosophy. Discuss the climate. Discuss the ground. Discuss the leadership. Discuss military methods.	The winning factors	
2	It starts with your military philosophy. Command your people in a way that gives them a shared higher purpose. You can lead them to death. You can lead them to life. They must never fear danger or dishonesty.	The Moral Law	
2, 3	Next is the commander. He must be smart, trustworthy, caring, brave, and strict.	Qualities of the commander	
2	You have your military methods. They shape your organization. They come from your management philosophy. You must master their use.	Methods and disciplines	
2	Next, you have the climate. It can be sunny or overcast. It can be hot or cold. It includes the timing of the seasons.	Timing	
2	Next is the terrain. It can be distant or near. It can be difficult or easy. It can be open or narrow. It also determines your life and death.	Location	
2	All five of these factors are critical. As a commander, you must pay attention to them. Understanding them means victory. Ignoring them means defeat.	The winning factors	
3	This is war. It is the most important skill in the nation. It is the basis of life and death. It is the philosophy of survival or destruction. You must know it well.	Defining problems	
3	Victory comes from knowing when to attack and when to avoid battle. Victory comes from correctly using both large and small forces. Victory comes from everyone sharing the same goals. Victory comes from finding opportunities in problems. Victory comes from having a capable commander and the government leaving him alone. You must know these five things.	Leader's vision and mission	

3	You must learn through planning. You must question the situation. Some commanders perform this analysis. If you use these commanders, you will win. Keep them. Some commanders ignore this analysis. If you use these commanders, you will lose. Get rid of them.	Planning and analysis
3	Use a cup of the enemy's food. It is worth twenty of your own. Win a bushel of the enemy's feed. It is worth twenty of your own.	Managing resources
3	All successful armies require thousands of men. They invade and march thousands of miles. Whole families are destroyed. Other families must be heavily taxed. Everyday, a large amount of money must be spent. Internal and external events force people to move. They are unable to work while on the road. They are unable to find and hold useful job. This affects seventy thousands of families.	Managing resources
3	Some leaders are generous but cannot use their men. They love their men but cannot command them. Their men are unruly and disorganized. Their soldiers are useless.	Managing personnel
3	Manage your government correctly at the start of a war. Close your borders and tear up passports. Block the passage of envoys. Encourage politicians at headquarters to stay out of it. You must use any means to put an end to politics.	Community partnership and politics
4	Some field positions are unobstructed. Some field positions are entangling. Some field positions are supporting. Some field positions are constricted. Some field positions give you a barricade. Some field positions are spread out.	Position analysis
4	The rules for making war are: If you outnumber enemy forces winning ten to one, surround them. If you outnumber them five to one, attack them. If you outnumber them two to one, divide them. If you are equal, then find an advantageous battle. If you are fewer, defend against them. If you are much weaker, evade them.	Seeking winning positions
4	Creating a winning war is like balancing a coin of gold against a coin of silver. Creating a losing war is like balancing a coin of silver against a coin of gold.	Seeking winning positions

(continues)

Table 7.2. (continued)

4	See the time to move. Don't try to find something clever. Hear the clap of thunder. Don't try to hear something subtle.	Seeking wining positions
4	This is the art of war: Discuss the distances. Discuss your numbers. Discuss your calculations. Discuss your decisions. Discuss victory. The ground determines the distance. The distance determines your numbers. Your numbers determine your calculations. Your calculations determine your decisions. Your decisions determine your victory.	Making calculated decisions
4	You make war using a deceptive position. If you use deception, then you can move. Using deception, you can upset the enemy and change the situation.	Deception strategies
4	Attack when you have a surplus of strength. Move your forces when you have a clear advantage.	Attack strategies
4	You win in battle by getting the opportunity to attack.	Attack strategies
5	You can speak and you will not be heard. You must use gongs and drums. You cannot really see your forces by looking. You must use banners and flags. You must master gong, drums, banners, and flags. In night battle, you must use numerous fires and drums. In day battles, you must use many banners and flags. You must position your people to control what they see and hear.	Communication strategies
5	You control a large group the same as you control a few. You just divide their ranks correctly. You fight a large army the same as you fight a small one. You only need the right position and communication.	Large group communication strategies
5	You must master gongs, drums, banners, and flags. Place people as a single unit where they all see and hear. You must unite them as one. The brave cannot advance alone. The fearful cannot withdraw alone. You must force them to act as a group.	Unity through communication
5	You must always know the enemy's situation. You can obtain foreknowledge. You can't get it from demons and spirits. You can't see it from professional experience. You can't check it with analysis. You can only get it from other people.	Foreknowledge strategies

5	Be a smart commander and a good general. You do this by using your best and brightest people for spying. This is how you achieve the greatest success. This is how you meet the necessities of war. The whole army's position and ability to move depends on these spies.	Sources of foreknowledge	
5	You need a creative leader and a worthy commander. You must move your troops to the right places to beat others. You must accomplish your attack and escape unharmed. This requires foreknowledge.	Sources of foreknowledge	
5	When there is much running about and the soldiers fall into rank. It means that the crucial moment has come. When the soldiers stand leaning on their spears, they are faint from want of food. The sight of men whispering together in small knots or speaking in subdued tones point to disaffection amongst the rank and file.	Nonverbal communication strategies	
5	You go hundreds of miles to fight for an advantage. Then the enemy catches your commanders and your army. Your strong soldiers get there first. Your weaker soldiers follow behind. Using this approach, only one in ten will arrive. You can try to go fifty miles to fight for an advantage. Then your commander and army will stumble. Using this method, only half of your soldiers will make it. You can try to go thirty miles to fight for an advantage. Then only two out of three get there. If you make your army travel without good supply lines, your army will die. Without supplies and food, your army will die. If you don't save the harvest, your army will die.	Setting goals	
6	Know yourself and know your enemy. You will be safe in every battle. You might know yourself but not know the enemy. You will then lose one battle for every one you win. You might not know yourself or the enemy. You will then lose every battle.	Analyzing self, people, and problem	
7	When you form your strategy, know the strengths and weaknesses of your plan.	Planning for strengths and weaknesses	
7	Manage your military position like water. Water takes every shape. It avoids the high and moves to the low. Your war can take any shape. It must avoid the strong and strike the weak. Water follows the shape of the land that directs its flow.	Understanding weaknesses and strengths	

CONCLUSION

In 500 B.C., Sun Tzu, a brilliant Chinese military general, wrote a dissertation about the importance of war to the preservation and prosperity of the state. The *Art of War* discusses leadership strategies and their application. The role of the general is most crucial, according to Sun Tzu, because the road to winning wars involves effective leadership. Sun Tzu's leadership strategies are very broad, and they are succinctly conceptualized in the study of the five winning factors. A good understanding of the five factors requires more than just reading them; one must personally experience the intricate balance of the leadership factors with the yin and yang of the environment. The effective leader must understand a situation well to balance the three internal factors of leader, philosophy, and methods, and the two external factors of climate and ground.

In 1859, Horace Mann, the father of American education, in his final address to the graduating class of Antioch College in Ohio said "Be ashamed to die until you have won some victory for humanity" (Cremin 1957). Victory for humanity involves inevitable changes, and education is a vehicle of change, with educational leaders driving it. Being educational leaders has not been rewarding, because they are seldom praised and rarely honored. However, we are confident that when the final chapter of the book of humanity is written, it will be about education and educational leaders who will have contributed to society by improving human equality, justice, and dignity.

In the United States, the survival and destruction of a nation with reference to the improvement of education are well documented in a Nation at Risk, Goals 2000, and the No Child Left Behind Act. The course of improving education over the past decades has literally been like going through wars. If educators are to win some victory for humanity to ensure the prosperity of the nation, they must first understand and redirect themselves and other people from self-interest to the public good, from violence to harmony, from bigotry to tolerance, and last but not least, from ignorance to knowledge. We hope this book inspires you to study and apply the concepts of effective leadership, and most of all to understand and refine your own leadership practices to win for our children.

REFERENCES

Cremin, Lawrence. 1957. *The republic and the school: Horace Mann on the education of free men.* New York: Teachers College Press.

ABOUT THE AUTHOR

Ovid K. Wong is currently an associate education professor at Benedictine University in Lisle, Illinois. He received his B.Sc. from the University of Alberta, his M.Ed. from the University of Washington, and his Ph.D. in curriculum and instruction from the University of Illinois. His experience in public education spans more than twenty years, from the urban classroom to the suburban office of the assistant school superintendent. In 1989, Dr. Wong received the National Science Foundation's Outstanding Science Teacher in Illinois award and the National Science Teaching Achievement Recognition (STAR) award from the National Science Teachers Association. In the same year, he visited the former Soviet Union as the environmental science delegation leader with the student ambassador program. He was the first recipient of the outstanding alumni award from the University of Alberta in 1992 and also the first recipient of the distinguished alumni award from the College of Education at the University of Illinois in 1995. He is the author of twenty-one books and has received the Midwest Book Author award from the Children's Reading Roundtable of Chicago. His most recent twelve books are dedicated to coaching teachers and students to effectively prepare for the state-mandated examination in Illinois, Michigan, and Ohio. Dr. Wong is married with two adult children.